S0-BJA-435

A LITTLE BIT

OF

MANTRAS

A LITTLE BIT
OF
MANTRAS

AN INTRODUCTION TO
SACRED SOUNDS

LILY CUSHMAN

STERLING ETHOS

New York

STERLING ETHOS
New York

An Imprint of Sterling Publishing Co., Inc.
1166 Avenue of the Americas
New York, NY 10036

ISBN 978-1-4549-3373-1

Distributed in Canada by Sterling Publishing Co., Inc.
c/o Canadian Manda Group, 664 Annette Street
Toronto, Ontario M6S 2C8, Canada
Distributed in the United Kingdom by GMC Distribution Services
Castle Place, 166 High Street, Lewes, East Sussex BN7 1XU, England
Distributed in Australia by NewSouth Books
University of New South Wales, Sydney, NSW 2052, Australia

For information about custom editions, special sales, and premium and corporate purchases,
please contact Sterling Special Sales at 800-805-5489 or specialsales@sterlingpublishing.com.

Manufactured in Canada

2 4 6 8 10 9 7 5 3 1

sterlingpublishing.com

Interior design by Gina Bonanno
Cover design by Elizabeth Mihaltse Lindy

Author Photo Credit: Elena Gorelik
iStock: INDECraft: 57; Shutterstock: handini_atmodiwiryo: 30; Elchin Jafarli:
cover, throughout; Katika: 27, 32, 35, 39, 79, 105; MapensStudio: cover,
throughout; Samburova Maria: 21, 30; VectorPot: cover, throughout
Mantra Illustrations by Charlie Cox

CONTENTS

INTRODUCTION

What are mantras? For thousands of years, the sacred sounds of mantras have been used to unlock the vast potential of the human heart and mind. These powerful tools can be found in cultures around the globe, offering accessible methods for healing, discovery, and well-being. I first came across mantras in my early twenties while I was living in the wilds of New York City's East Village, working as a full-time musician and recording engineer. My introduction to mantras came after a deeply tumultuous time in my life, marked by the deaths of several immediate family members and the attacks of September 11. For many years I was shattered by the events of this time, trying to piece together a sense of wholeness and understanding. I experimented with many modalities of healing and transformation, seeking a new orientation to life that I am still discovering to this day.

My introduction to mantras came during this period and evoked a deep resonance in me. I would have never thought doing something as simple or weird as reciting words in another language could have such a profound effect on my life—but they have. I have always felt at home in mantras. They have soothed me when nothing else would. They enabled me to walk through life more genuinely connected to myself and others. Over the past decade, they have become a cornerstone for me, a lifeline to the deepest parts of myself, and a means to learn how to live authentically from those places.

It has taken me many years to translate and understand the essence of this practice from its roots in Hindu philosophy, and skillfully apply it to my own life. This book is a synthesis of that exploration, and I hope it will jump-start your own journey into sacred sounds.

The book begins with the history of mantras from different traditions around the world and a look at my own lineage of Bhakti Yoga. We'll investigate the many benefits of mantra practice on the brain and the body through recent scientific studies, substantiating what monks and yogis have contended for centuries. Next, we'll examine the core framework of practice methodology, which includes speaking, singing, and writing practice. Then we'll dive into the mantras themselves, introducing thirteen Sanskrit mantras from the Hindu tradition. Each mantra breakdown includes:

❀ **Pronunciation Guide**

❀ **Benefits**

❀ **Associated Deity**

❀ **Literal Meaning**

❀ **Mythology and Folklore**

❀ **Practical Application**

❀ **Recommended Practices**

There is also a supplemental practice companion that accompanies this book, with audio and visual resources to support your home practice. Lastly, you'll learn creative ways to apply mantra practice on a daily basis with specific techniques for working with anxiety, negative emotions, challenging situations, health and healing, bringing intention to your routine, and more.

A Little Bit of Mantras is an in-depth introduction to the origins of sacred sounds for anyone interested in putting them into regular practice. The methods spelled out in this book have changed my life, giving me a comprehensive skill set to live with ease, humor, and joy, no matter what comes my way. So, whether you are brand-new to mantras or looking to expand your existing practice, get ready to go on a journey exploring the rich and expansive world of sacred sounds—and the vast power they have to unlock our deepest potential.

1

WHAT ARE MANTRAS? THE HISTORY OF SACRED SOUND

MANTRAS ARE SACRED SOUNDS OR SACRED syllables. When repeated with dedication and focus, mantras serve as a means to steady the mind and open the heart. The word *mantra* originates from the Sanskrit language and was adopted into the English language in the late eighteenth century. The word can be broken into two roots, *man* and *tra*. *Man* is associated with the root for the word *manas*, which means "mind." *Tra* is defined as "crossing over." Combined, the literal translation of the word *mantra* is "crossing over the mind." But what exactly does it mean to cross over the mind? What lies on the other side? And why would anyone want to go there? This whole concept is quite foreign to Western culture, except when we desperately want to get rid of a migraine! However, in the traditions of the East, seekers have been exploring practices to learn how to work with the mind for thousands of years, in search of greater happiness and well-being.

These traditions believe that "crossing over the mind" allows us to gain access to the fullness of our being. Beyond our anxiety, distraction, and fearfulness lies a vast potential for greater connection, creativity, and curiosity. This is what awaits us in the world of mantras: an immense toolkit that enables us to inhabit our lives.

Since being adopted into the English language, the word *mantra* has taken on a broader meaning from its roots in Hindu culture. The Oxford English Dictionary primarily defines *mantra* as "a word or sound repeated to aid concentration in meditation."[1] This definition is not far from the traditional meaning, in that meditation is another way of describing "crossing over the mind." However, a second definition is also given for the word, which is quite different from the traditional meaning of the word: "a statement or slogan repeated frequently." This second definition speaks more to the common usage of the word in Western culture, which is more akin to an affirmation or a motto. This colloquial usage is actually an incomplete application of the word. In a truer sense of the word, a mantra is a very precise sound frequency, language, rhythm, and even cadence that unlocks specific energies and qualities in the practitioner. An affirmation, on the other hand, can be any word or statement in your native language that reinforces a belief or motto of some kind. To get a better understanding of the potency of sacred sounds, let's look at the history of mantras from their primary home in Hindu culture, and where else they show up across the world.

MANTRAS IN HINDU TRADITION

Mantras are part of a much larger body of ritual, teaching, and practice that make up the traditional Hindu philosophy. This tradition is so ancient that it's difficult to nail down an exact time line of its origins. As in most cultures, these earliest traditions were passed down aurally from teacher to student for generations before there were any written records. The earliest written record of mantras in the Hindu tradition can be found in the Vedas, a group of ancient Sanskrit texts. These texts are the oldest written records of the Indo-Iranian culture. Hindus consider these texts to be "authorless"[2] or "not of man."[3] The dates of these texts are quite controversial, with scholars citing their origins as dating anywhere from three thousand to seven thousand years ago. This gives a time frame for how long these mantras have been in use, but it doesn't answer the question of where the mantras come from. Most Hindus consider mantras to be the songs of the rishis, the greatest saints and sages of ancient India. Hindu folklore credits the creation of the universe to a singular primordial mantra, noting that the mantra existed before any other matter in the universe. So the actual source of mantras is quite mystical, which makes it all the more impressive that they have been in use for thousands of years!

Mantras are practiced in many different spiritual lineages under the umbrella of Hindu traditions. In Bhakti Yoga, mantras are used to cultivate devotion as a path to open the heart and consciousness.

In Nāda Yoga, mantras are part of a system of transformation of the body and mind through inner and outer sounds. Kriya Yoga uses mantras, along with breathing and mudra practice, to enter deep states of stillness. Laya Yoga uses mantras as well as breathing, yoga postures, mudras, and bandhas to awaken kundalini in the body to experience higher states of consciousness. The rich and diverse usage of mantras throughout these many branches has also spilled over into mainstream pop culture. When traveling the streets of Delhi, you can see mantras incorporated in the names of businesses, such as buildings made from Guru Bricks or Om India Hydraulic Hoses. Even better, your tiny rickshaw is usually covered in mantras bumper stickers and fully decorated with deities galore. Mantras are integral to everyday life in the Hindu tradition, both in focused spiritual practice, and as a part of the rich landscape of Indian culture.

MANTRAS AROUND THE WORLD

Aside from the Hindu tradition, mantras have a diverse history, spanning many cultures and religions around the world. Throughout civilization, prayer and song have always been a channel for connection and expanding the heart and mind. These expressions range from the formal systems that govern many organized religions to the simpler sounds that parents use to communicate with their infants. In other Eastern traditions, such as Buddhism, Jainism, Sikhism, and Taoism, mantras play a significant role. Mantras are also used in Judaism, Christianity, Paganism, and many shamanic traditions. Here are some different mantras from different faiths around the world.

FROM THE BUDDHIST TRADITION:

Om Mani Padme Hum (I bow to the jewel in the lotus of the heart)

Nam myoho renge kyo (Homage to the lotus sutra)

Sabbe sattā sukhi hontu (May all beings be happy)

Gate gate paragate parasaāgate bodhi svaha (Gone, gone, gone beyond, gone utterly beyond, O what an awakening)

FROM THE CHRISTIAN TRADITION:

Lord Jesus Christ, have mercy on me

Hail Mary, full of grace

FROM THE JAIN TRADITION:

Namokar mantra (bowing down to the conquerors of the senses)

Pratikramana prayer (asking for forgiveness)

FROM THE JEWISH TRADITION:

Shema Yisrael Adonai Eloheinu, Adonai Echad (Hear O Israel: The Sovereign our God, the Sovereign is One)

Shalom (Peace)

Elohim (a name for God)

FROM THE MUSLIM TRADITION:

    Allahu Akbar (God is great)

    *Bismillah Al-Rahman, Al-Rahim (*In the name of God, most Gracious, most Compassionate)

FROM THE SIKH TRADITION:

    Wahe Guru (wonderful teacher)

    Mool Mantra (basic teaching)

Indigenous peoples around the world have also used mantras in a variety of healing and ceremonial practices for centuries, as have shamans in Native American culture. Polynesian culture, too, has a history with sacred sounds, as do aboriginal Australians, and Mayan and Incan civilizations. Mantras are found in all these different faiths, traditions, and cultures, leading us to recognize the universality of this practice.

CONCLUSION

One of my favorite origin myths about mantras is related to their origin as being heard by ancient rishis (or sages) of India. Rishis were thought to be "seers" of truth" who were so in tune with the divine nature of life, that they would hear the mantras as the fabric of the cosmos. It was thought that these mantras were already in existence in an un-manifested form, and that the rishis were merely hearing them.

I love this concept that sacred sounds are all around us, and accessible to everyone, like a flowing river, just waiting to be heard. By reciting a mantra, it is as though we were tapping into an ancient current that thousands before us have also entered into, as a means of discovery and transformation. Our mantra practice can be a continuation of the many seekers who have come before us, and the many more who will follow us.

THE BENEFITS OF MANTRA: WHAT SCIENCE SAYS

WITH THE RISE OF YOGA AND MINDFULNESS practices over the past several decades, there has been an increase in scientific studies assessing the measurable effects that these practices have on the mind and body. These research studies reveal the fascinating science behind what the fans of mantra practice have been touting for thousands of years: that mantras change us from the inside out. The benefits of this ancient practice include a healthy body, a healthy brain, mental well-being, and emotional well-being. In this chapter, we'll explore the broader benefits that mantras offer. In the second half of the book, we'll take a more specific look at the unique benefits that individual mantras have on a case-by-case basis.

MANTRA OR NOT?

One of the most common questions new students ask is if there is a benefit to chanting a mantra compared to chanting a nonmantra. A 2017 study compared the difference with twenty-one Buddhist practitioners.[1] In the study, participants were shown either a neutral photo or a negative photo to induce stress and/or fear. In either case, the participants were instructed to mentally repeat the mantra for the Buddha or the name "Santa Claus." Electroencephalography (EEG) was used to measure activity in different parts of the brain. The baseline for the study was the difference in the brain modulation between the participant being shown a neutral photo and a negative photo. Then participants were shown either a neutral photo or a negative photo while mentally repeating either the mantra or "Santa Claus" to compare the effect of each. When participants repeated "Santa Claus" after being shown a negative photo there was no change in the modulation of the brain. But when they repeated the mantra, the brain responded as though they were seeing the neutral photo, even though they were looking at the negative photo. This finding reveals that the effect of mantras may not be the same as that of an ordinary word. So there is much greater benefit in repeating an actual mantra than in simply a random word.

The Relaxation Response

One of the earliest investigators of the science of mantra was Herbert Benson, a cardiologist and professor of mind/body medicine at Harvard Medical School. Dr. Benson was the founder of the Mind/Body Medical Institute at Massachusetts General Hospital, where he is also the director emeritus of the Benson-Henry Institute. Dr. Benson's early work focused on building awareness of the connection between mind and body in Western medicine. Before the 1960s, doctors virtually ignored the mind-body connection in our culture. Dr. Benson's research approached the body and mind as one system, exploring how various practices, like yoga, meditation, mantra, and prayer, play a significant role in reducing the stress response. In his research, Dr. Benson coined the term *relaxation response* to scientifically describe the meditative state brought on by these practices. He defines the relaxation response as the opposite of the stress response of the body, also known as the *fight-or-flight response*. More specifically, the *relaxation response* is characterized by a set of physiological changes that include decreased oxygen consumption, decreased carbon dioxide elimination, a lower respiratory rate, increased brain cortical thickness, increased low-frequency heart rate oscillations, increased exhaled nitric oxide, and more.

In 2018, a study conducted by researchers at the Benson-Henry Institute further explored the effects of the *relaxation response* on stage 1 hypertension patients as adjunct therapy to anti-hypertensive drug therapy. The study revealed that blood pressure was reduced in over half of all patients after an eight-week relaxation response training, and the training was associated with improvements in psychological variables and specific changes in gene expression. "This is the first study to test such an intervention for a population of unmedicated adults with carefully documented persistent hypertension, and the first study to identify genomic determinants associated with the impact of a mind-body intervention on hypertension. Results from this study provide new insights into how integrative medicine, especially mind-body approaches, influences blood pressure control at the molecular level."[2]

The results of the study also show that the relaxation response practices may reduce inflammatory processes and promote immune functions, both of which contribute to blood pressure reduction in patients. However, even more exciting in this research is the evidence of how the relaxation response practices (mantra, yoga, meditation, and breathing techniques) may reduce blood pressure by altering the expression of the genes in a select set of biological pathways. This alteration of a DNA sequence is something that previously was only thought possible through birth, however, the study of epigenetics now reveals that environmental changes like stress, diet, pollution, and lifestyles all have the ability to affect what genes in our DNA are expressed, and passed on to our children. "This means that altered gene expression profiles in a parent could be inherited by their children and grandchildren which would have direct implications for health because it means individuals could develop a disease depending on the environment their parent or grandparent was exposed to even if they weren't exposed to it themselves."[3] In other words, your chanting practice will not only help your own blood pressure, but potentially also your children and grandchildren!

Lower Blood Pressure

Another promising study about the effects of chanting on blood pressure was done in 2008 by a senior lecturer in neuroscience at the Imperial College London. Dr. Alan Watkins conducted the study monitoring blood pressure and heart rate of five monks over a period of twenty-four hours. Results of the study revealed that both heart rate and blood pressure were at their lowest through the day while the monks were singing Gregorian chants. "We have recently carried out research that demonstrates that the regular breathing and musical structure of chanting can have a significant and positive physiological impact," says Dr. Alan Watkins.[4]

The Power of Om

In 2010 a study was conducted on the effects of the mantra Aum by the Indian Council of Medical Research Centre for Advanced Research in Yoga and Neurophysiology in Bangalore, India. Study participants were a group of experienced mantra practitioners with five to twenty years of experience. Each subject was studied in two different sessions, one using mantra meditation, and one with no targeted thinking. The study found "a combination of mental alertness with physiological rest during the practice of Om meditation."[5]

A 2018 study found similar results in the chanting of Aum for thirty minutes among a group of new meditators. The EEG was recorded before, during, and after the experiment, and researchers reported that an "increase in theta power was found after meditation when averaged across all brain regions."[6] Theta waves are thought to be present when individuals are in a state of deep mental relaxation or are engaged in creative endeavors promoting states of hyperfocus (due to a lack of distraction). Both of these studies suggest that Om meditation may increase relaxation by boosting this quiet state of focus.

Decreased Self-Referencing

Aside for the physiological benefits of mantra practice, numerous studies confirm the effect this practice has on the way we think. One brain network that has been found to be affected by mantra practice is the default mode network (DMN). Regions of the DMN are active when people engage in self-related thought, including memories and stories we have about ourselves, the description we have of ourselves, and our emotional reflection of ourselves.[7] In other words, the DMN is often activated by "me-related" thinking. Nodes of the DMN are also active when the mind wanders, remembering the past or thinking about the future. According to a 2017 study, "Training in mantra meditation, like other practices such as focused attention and open monitoring, also [had] a suppressive effect on activity within the DMN"[8] during a two-week study using kundalini mantra meditation. This finding reveals that in as little as two weeks' time, mantra practice will reduce brain activity that is often seen in self-centered thinking. This study supports the view that mantra practice can help reduce the obsessive thinking we often get lost in while telling ourselves stories about ourselves, as well as ruminating over the past and anxiously pondering the future.

Increased Resilience

One of the most powerful skills mantra practice cultivates is resilience. Resilience is our ability to get up when we fall, dust ourselves off, and start over. Mantra practice is not the only place we cultivate this skill directly; it's also a skill that's built into a variety of meditation and yoga modalities. Even though this benefit isn't unique to mantra practice, it is quite significant and has been validated with scientific research. In a 2012 study, Dr. Richie Davidson did an experiment at the Center for Healthy Minds at the University of Wisconsin–Madison on the effects of meditation when dealing with pain. In Davidson's study, researchers applied heat to the inside of the forearm, below the wrist, on a group of expert meditators, with over ten thousand hours of practice, and a group of novice meditators. "In each trial, subjects were given forty-five seconds to settle into a meditation state, then were presented with warm heat, a cue that the real heat was coming. Immediately afterward, participants' brains were scanned with a functional MRI.[9] The results showed something very interesting, according to the researchers: "The pain didn't bother the experts as much as it bothered the novices, in whom the anxiety of anticipation was stronger." The brain activity in the expert meditators showed that they more rapidly returned to a neutral resting state after the pain, and the novices would stay in a state of anticipatory anxiety about the pain, which is some cases was worse than the pain itself. In other words, the expert meditators had greater resilience in response to pain. These expert meditators were able to rest following the moment of pain, and, overall, handled the entire experience better as a result, even though the actual experience of the pain was the same for all participants, both experts and novices. The study points to the importance of cultivating the skill of resilience, learned through mantra practice and other modalities, so that we can better handle difficult situations by changing the way we relate to them.

Fighting Alzheimer's Disease

The Alzheimer's Research and Prevention Foundation in Tucson, Arizona has been studying the effects of mantra practice as a key element in an integrative approach to preventing memory loss and Alzheimer's since 1998. A 2017 study, conducted by researchers at the foundation, explored the effects of mantra practice and Kundalini Yoga on participants over the age of fifty-five with mild cognitive impairment.[10] The randomized groups were initially tested to establish baselines for cognitive understanding (that is, memory and executive functioning) and emotional intelligence (including depression, apathy, and resilience). They were checked once again at twelve weeks and twenty-four weeks. Half the group participated in a daily mantra and yoga practice, consisting of twelve minutes of daily mantra chanting, twelve minutes of prescribed breathing practice, and fifteen minutes of guided meditation. Half the group doing this daily practice "showed significant improvement in executive functioning and improvement in depressive symptoms and resilience after twelve and twenty-four weeks' time, as well as even longer-lasting benefits. These findings show exciting potential for a preventive approach to dementia and Alzheimer's disease that is just beginning to be explored with present-day scientific research.

In conclusion, there is growing scientific support for the benefits of sacred sounds. Whether your interest in mantras stems from simple curiosity or a desire for greater peace of mind, mantras offer a myriad of benefits for mind, body, and spirit. Now that we know more about the different ways that mantras benefit us, let's shift gears and look at how to go about working with them as an actual practice.

WHAT IS MANTRA PRACTICE?

NOW THAT WE UNDERSTAND THE MANY WAYS mantras can affect us, let's take a look at the nuts and bolts of putting them into formal practice. This practice is grounded in the lineage from which it comes, but we're applying it in a very modern and practical way. Don't worry if you don't connect with the mythology of the Hindu pantheon. That's not necessary to do this practice. For many years, I practiced mantra on a daily basis without knowing what I was saying, because I just liked how it felt to do the practice. Only years later did I start to explore the deeper meaning of the mantras and the folklore surrounding them. I encourage you to explore this practice in the way that feels more natural to you. Take the tools with you that you find helpful and leave behind what doesn't resonate with you.

MANTRA PRACTICE: A PRIMER

Mantra practice is the repetition of a sacred sound, either through speaking, singing, or writing. Mantra practice can be thought of as a skills training for our hearts and minds. Repeating a mantra seems deceivingly simple; however, this practice can revolutionize the way you relate to yourself and the world around you. By practicing mantras regularly, you will learn how to focus your attention, let go of distractions, and build resilience. The mantras themselves allow you to shift how you pay attention.

A key element to any practice—whether you're learning how to play chess, play baseball, or speak a new language—is repetition. In mantra practice, repetition is essential to slowly train you to pay attention differently. It doesn't happen overnight; in fact, teachers recommend that the most effective way to approach to mantra practice is a little every day, even if it's only five minutes while you sit in your car before walking in to work. One reason that repetition is essential for this practice stems from the way our brains are wired, and the science of how we create new habits and pathways in the brain.

HOW DO YOU PRACTICE MANTRAS?

There is a core framework for practice that is the same, no matter what type of mantra practice you are doing. Once you understand this framework, you can apply it to all different kinds of practice, as well as meditation or yoga. The structure of practice can be broken down into four steps:

1. **GATHERING YOUR ATTENTION INTO THE MANTRA**
2. **NOTICING WHEN YOUR MIND WANDERS**
3. **GENTLY LETTING GO OF THE DISTRACTION**
4. **BEGINNING AGAIN BY BRINGING YOUR ATTENTION BACK TO THE MANTRA**

Each step has its own nuance and function, so we'll take a look at each one individually.

1. Gathering Your Attention

The first step in this process is gathering yourself. You're moving from a scattered, fragmented state to one of focus and wholeness. This process is usually described as the cultivation of concentration, but I think of it more as herding cats in my mind. Most people assume that when we sit down to practice, it means we're going to magically force our minds to stop thinking, but that isn't how it works. What we're actually doing in mantra practice is gathering all the fragmented thoughts and feelings roaming around in our minds, and focusing them into a chosen object, in this case the mantra. We gather ourselves and pour it all into the mantra itself. This could mean speaking the mantra aloud, silently repeating it, singing the mantra, or writing it down.

As you repeat this process over time, you gradually get better at herding those cats. You slowly build the capacity to gather yourself from farther-flung corners of your mind, and with more efficiency. You'll remain focused longer, with greater ease, and feel more at home with the mantra itself. This is what concentration looks like. It's like training for a marathon. You don't gain the ability to finish the marathon in one afternoon run, but rather gradually, over time. And once you build that concentration muscle, you can apply it to any facet of your life. You can singularly focus on a coworker telling you about her dream vacation, you can fully immerse yourself in giving your dog the haircut of a lifetime, you can wholeheartedly eat lunch with every part of your being. The power you build in mantra practice is an embodied form of concentration that enables you to go all-in on anything you do with no holding back. When I first started to feel the effects of higher concentration in my life, I discovered the amazing capacity to work on projects for endless hours at a time, without ever losing focus or interest. More than ever before, I could dive deeper into my work, accessing profound states of creativity, clarity and engagement with great ease, and feel more at home with the mantra itself. This is what concentration looks like. It's like training for a marathon. You don't gain the ability to finish the marathon in one afternoon run, but rather gradually, over time. And once you build that concentration muscle, you can apply it to any facet of your life. You can single-mindedly focus on a coworker telling you about her dream vacation, you can fully immerse yourself in giving your dog the haircut of a lifetime, you can wholeheartedly eat lunch with every part of your being. The power you build in mantra practice is an embodied form of concentration that enables you to go all-in on anything you do with no holding back. When I first started to feel the effects of higher concentration in my life, I could suddenly spend five hours writing some new music without once getting distracted. I would get so into whatever I was doing that most of the day would go by before I remembered to go to the bathroom or have a glass of water!

2. Noticing When Your Mind Wanders

Once we've gathered ourselves, the mind does what the mind does: it wanders. Remember, the point of this practice isn't to magically stop our thoughts. Instead, we're training ourselves to work differently with the mind. So, step two in this process is simply realizing that we've wandered—realizing that those cats are roaming free again. One moment you're with the mantra and, the next thing you know, you're ten minutes into picking out baby names for the daughter you're never going to have with the stranger from the gym who smiled at you yesterday. Ten minutes in. In other words, you've been gone for quite some time before you even realize it. That's what I call the *gap*. The gap is the space between the moment when you lose the concentration, and the moment when you realize you've lost it. This gap can last a few seconds or a few minutes, depending on how good you are at picking out baby names. What's befuddling about this is that the gap is out of our control—the whole thing happens under the radar. We're not actively choosing to let go of the mantra; it happens on its own—which is why many people become discouraged in practice. The majority of our scatteredness is totally out of our hands. But don't worry—we're not done yet, and what comes next is quite revolutionary.

3. Letting Go of Distraction

We step back into the driver's seat with step three: letting go. In reality, we could keep going and allow the distraction take us further down the rabbit hole. But we know that trajectory all too well. So instead of falling back into our default mode of chasing the distraction, we use the mantra to try a different tactic, the revolutionary act of letting go. Letting go is like saying *"not now"* to the distraction, instead of allowing it take us further away from our anchor in the practice. In other words, we let go of anything that *is not mantra*. This choice may seem pretty innocuous at first, but it is actually a really big deal to learn how to stand up against a lifetime of conditioning. Rarely are we taught the value of letting go, or how to do it. Instead, we're trained to hang on as tightly as possible to everyone and everything around us. The beauty of mantra practice is that it gives us a chance to try a different way of doing things, and to find out for ourselves what is useful and what ultimately keeps us moving forward.

4. Beginning Again with Mantra

Once we have let go, the last step is turning our attention back to the mantra to begin again. This final movement is about reconnecting back to home base and gathering there once again. This is essential for us to continue onward. Without it we aren't going to accomplish much of anything. Beginning again is like saying, "Oh wait, where was I? Oh yes, I was practicing mantra," and then picking it back up again. It's important to recognize this core movement of *wandering and coming back* in mantra practice because many newbies take it as a sign of failure. But *beginning again is the practice itself.* And when you can settle into the rhythm of being okay with wandering and beginning again, that is when you start to accomplish a lot. Personally, I love this step of the practice because it's the most empowering. No matter what happens, we can always rise from the ashes and begin again. Even after the biggest detours in life, this step teaches us that we can recover and continue onward with what matters most to us. And what greater power could we have in life than that? So once again this skill we are working with on the micro level is serving us on the macro level of our lives in a significant way. To quote world renowned meditation teacher, Sharon Salzberg, "The healing is in the return, not in never having wandered to begin with."

This four-step framework for practice is a cyclical process, meaning you will do it over and over again. In other words, being awesome at mantra practice doesn't mean that you only run through this four-step process once in a sitting and then never do it again. Learning how to be successful in this practice is learning how to go through these four steps efficiently and with ease—as many times as you find yourself distracted. The goal is not to engage in this process fewer times; the goal is to do the process as effectively as possible. Practitioners who have been practicing mantras for fifty years still go through this same process, but they do it with more patience and compassion. They can let go of distractions more easily, they don't get lost in their self-judgment for as long, and they can begin again more quickly and with greater enthusiasm.

Now that you know the nuts and bolts of what mantra practice involves, and the skills we learn from doing it, let's explore the three core methods for mantra practice that you'll be using to apply this framework.

PRO TIP:

The art of beginning again also applies to our practice as a whole. Everyone has periods of regular daily practice that drop off when life gets busy. Any long-term practitioner will tell you that learning how to return to daily practice after losing momentum is the secret to success. So instead of beating yourself up for not maintaining a daily practice, try framing the moment as an opportunity to reconnect to the deeper motivation of your practice by simply beginning again.

❖ 4 ❖

FORMAL MANTRA PRACTICE

THERE ARE THREE PRIMARY METHODS OF FORMAL mantra practice: speaking, singing, and writing. Each of these have been in use for thousands of years in the Hindu tradition. The anchor for each practice is the mantra itself, but each one features a different approach, depending on the practitioner's individual learning style. The spoken and singing practice both work best for auditory learners, while the written practice supports visual and reading/writing learners. Each method is equally effective and stands on its own as a complete practice, so I recommend trying each one to find the method that best suits you.

METHODS OF MANTRA PRACTICE

Japa: speaking mantra aloud or silently

Kirtan: singing mantra

Likhita Japa: writing or drawing mantra

Japa जप: Speaking Mantra

Japa practice is the method of speaking a mantra aloud or silently. The mantra can be spoken loudly, in a soft whisper, or repeated silently. The Sanskrit word *japa* is derived from the root *jap*, which means "to utter in a low voice, repeat internally, mutter."[1] In japa, practice anchoring your awareness to the spoken words of the mantra, and hearing yourself say the mantra. Japa mantra practice is best suited to auditory learners.

In this method, the mantra is repeated a specific number of times, or in sets of specific numbers. The most common number for japa practice is 108 repetitions (an auspicious number in the Hindu tradition) or, for longer mantras, odd numbers like 3, 11, or 13. The counting of mantra repetitions is most often done using mala prayer beads, similar to the way a rosary is used. A traditional necklace mala has 108 beads plus 1 head bead (the sumera or guru bead), and the bracelet mala has 27 beads plus 1 head bead (so that four rounds on the bracelet equal 108 recitations). Malas are made from many different materials, including wood, seeds, and semiprecious stones. Over time, a mala gradually becomes imbued with the properties of the mantra it's used with counting, so it's common to only use one mantra for a single mala, and to use that mala for many years. Malas are a little impractical for longer mantras, so there are other counting mechanisms employed in such cases, like thirteen small stones in a bowl, or a handheld tally counter.

One of the things I love about japa practice is how portable and unobtrusive it is. If you have a mala, you can slip it into your pocket and take your formal practice anywhere. You can do this practice without a ton of equipment, a special outfit, or anyone thinking you're superweird. And for those of us whose daily schedule is erratic, the portability of this method makes it more conducive for daily use. When we can't find time at home, we can sneak ten minutes on the subway during rush hour, during a lunchtime walk, or wherever we can realistically find the time.

PRO TIP:
HOW TO USE A MALA?

Hold your mala in your right hand, resting the beads over your middle finger and gently point your index finger away from you. Starting with the head bead, pull the mala toward you, one bead at a time, using your thumb. When you complete a full circle around the mala, do not cross over the head bead. Instead, turn the mala around so that your next round moves in the opposite direction. Continue each round in this manner, first clockwise, and then counterclockwise.

Kirtan कीर्‌तन: Singing Mantra

Kirtan practice is the method of singing mantras, accompanied by music or acappella. Kirtan is most often done as a group practice, though is can also be done solo. The Sanskrit word kirtan means "calling out" or "praising." Like japa practice, this method is best suited to auditory learners, though kirtan tends to be more dynamic than japa, since it's a music-based practice. In this practice, the music has a beautiful way of drawing us back to the mantra, or, as Krishna Das says, "The medicine of the Name [the mantra] is hidden in the sugar syrup of music."[2]

In a group setting, this method is call-and-response singing between the kirtan leader and the group. The leader starts by singing the mantra (the call), and the group then responds by singing the mantra back (the response). The anchor for your attention in this method toggles between listening to the mantra (being sung by the leader) and then singing the mantra yourself. At first it can feel pretty weird to sing mantras with a bunch of strangers, but there are some incredible benefits to doing this practice in a group setting. Think of the last concert you went to, and what it felt like to sing your favorite song along with the rest of the audience; there's great power in collective action, especially when aimed at such a positive force as mantras. Oftentimes, group kirtans swell with energy, inspiring some practitioners to dance ecstatically, while others experience a depth of peace and calm that is otherwise inaccessible. Kirtan practice can also be done solo by singing along to recordings of chanting, or, for the musically inclined, singing on your own while playing different instruments.

Many traditional mantra melodies have been sung for thousands of years as part of this practice. In modern Hindu culture, there are singers and musicians who sing haunting renditions of popular mantras, like unforgettable love songs. In Indian culture, the singing of kirtan is suffused with the mythology of the Hindu pantheon, which has a very romantic sensibility of calling to the Divine from a place of deep longing to connect with something much larger than ourselves. Kirtan practitioners are said to enter into states of *samadhi* (enlightenment) simply by wholeheartedly singing mantras.

PRO TIP:
PRACTICE IS NOT PERFORMANCE

Kirtan isn't a performance, it's a practice. Though it looks
similar to a musical performance, the focus is not on how
we sound, but how we pay attention to the mantra.
The mantras are a vehicle for paying attention differently.
Aside from learning the correct pronunciation of a mantra,
this isn't about sounding a certain way, so give yourself
permission to sing the mantras wholeheartedly without
worrying about how you sound.

Likhita Japa लखितजप: Writing Mantra

Likhita Japa is the method of drawing or writing mantras in Sanskrit. This form of practice is a way to fix your mind on a mantra through the act of writing, drawing, tracing, or coloring in the mantra in the original Sanskrit lettering. It works best for visual learners and reading/writing learners. The anchor in this method is the Sanskrit lettering of the mantra on the page. This written form of the lettering becomes the focal point for you to return your attention to each time your mind wanders during the practice. This method of mantra practice isn't as well know as speaking or singing; however, it can be equally powerful. Many Indian saints and yogis left behind journals after their death that were full of only one mantra, written thousands of times.

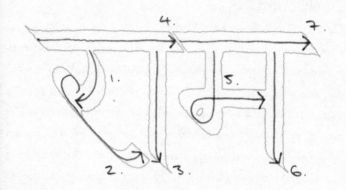

The Sanskrit alphabet is a very specific system for drawing letters that includes an exact order for each stroke of each letter. In the practice companion download of this book, you will find a writing guide for each mantra included in the book, as well a version of the mantra to trace and color in. This practice can also be done in groups, having art parties to draw or color in specific mantras themes. This method easily translates to less formal periods of practice, if you like drawing mantras while listening to music or relaxing on your commute.

See Resources (page 110) for the practice companion download for each mantra in this book.

CONCLUSION

These three core mantra methods are the most common traditional ways of doing mantra practice, but there are many additional ways to work with mantras, like walking practice, or a breath-based practice. All of these are considered "formal practices." Formal practice is space to step away from the usual flow of our lives and experiment with these methods in a deliberate and focused way. This means doing the practice without simultaneously doing eight other things. I recommend setting up a space in your home that is solely dedicated to your mantra practice, where you can be free of disruptions or distractions. In that space, you can really slow down enough to look at your mind and try out some new ways of being with yourself. No matter which core mantra method you are using, this is space in which you will learn the essential skills of letting go and beginning again. And once you gain some confidence in these methods, you'll find many ways to integrate mantra practice into the rest of your day in a more informal way.

Now that you have the nuts and bolts of the core methods for mantra practice, we'll dive into the mantras themselves: their meaning, mythology, and modern-day applications. We'll be exploring thirteen different mantras for you to begin working with. Each of these mantras has its own specific essence and awakens particular qualities and virtues. Let's go!

PRO TIP:
TAKE IT EASY

Practice in the easiest way possible. A practice is inherently challenging—we are learning new skills—so don't make it harder than it needs to be. Try to find a way to practice comfortably in both the physical and emotional sense. You can sit on the floor or in a chair; you can walk or lie down. No one body position is better than another, so find what works best for you!.

MANTRAS
FOR
PEACE

AUM

❋ **MANTRA:** Aum

❋ **PRONUNCIATION:** *ah-OH-mm*

❋ **BENEFITS:** Connection, tranquility

❋ **ASSOCIATED DEITIES:** The *trimurti* ("three forms") of Brahma, Vishnu, and Shiva

❋ **MEANING:** The primordial sound, the sound of the universe, the cosmic sound

❋ **MYTHOLOGY:** The mantra and written symbol of Aum (also commonly spelled Om) is one of the most sacred in the Hindu tradition. The exact date of origin of this mantra is difficult to pinpoint, but the earliest written record is usually placed around 1700–1100 BCE, making it older than the last living woolly mammoth!

In Hindu mythology, Aum is known as the primordial sound, and is at the center of one of the most common myths of creation. According to the folklore, before the existence of the cosmos, before space or time, all that existed was the potential for existence. Out of that possibility grew a subtle friction that evolved into a slight humming vibration. This humming gradually became the sound of Aum, and from that sound, the entire cosmos sprang into existence. So, it is thought that the sound of Aum is the very foundation of life itself, a sacred thread that is woven through the fabric of life. And by chanting Aum, we are connecting with the sound of the entire universe.

This mantra is broken down in four parts, each of which represent different qualities and aspects:

1. **A:** creation, Brahma, Jagrat (the waking state)
2. **U:** preservation, Vishnu, Swapna (dream state)
3. **M:** destruction, Shiva, Sushupti (dreamless sleep state)
4. **Silence after sound:** Turiya (transcendental space that pervades everything

The silence that follows the sound of Aum is considered to be as important as the **A-U-M** sound. Known as Turiya, this silence is considered to be pure consciousness that exists underneath all form. Turiya is also thought to transcend all of the waking, dreaming and dreamless states. Tuning into this silence can be a powerful way to experience this all-pervading potential that we are typically unaware of.

This mantra is so fundamental in Hindu practices that it is often used to start longer mantras, as you will see in many other mantras in this book. It is also found in other Eastern traditions of Buddhist, Jainism, and Sikhism, and has been related to many additional meanings and mythologies.

Application

In practical application, this mantra serves as a vehicle to connect with all of life around us in a palpable, direct way. In chanting Aum, we vibrate the body and the space around us with the sound. It is said that you can hear the sound of Aum vibrating all around us if you listen in a certain way, so, in chanting this mantra, we are joining the flow of a sound that is already there. In doing so, we can start to soften the boundaries that we so often feel between "me" and "not-me." The construct of separation begins to relax and instead of experiencing the differences between us and them, we can instead start to experience the commonality among us all—that we are all made of the same sound and vibration of Aum.

This mantra has a calming effect on the body and mind, while simultaneously energizing the system. A study conducted in 1995 explored the effects of chanting Aum on the autonomic function of the body and revealed that those chanting Aum displayed an increase in "mental alertness with physiological rest,"[1] as compared to the control group that did nontargeted thinking during the same period. This supports what yogis have experienced for thousands of years:

that the practice of Aum increases both tranquility and alertness to promote a calm sense of readiness.

Another great way to work with this mantra is by drawing the symbol of it or coloring it in. One of my initial mantra practices came through the practice of coloring in the symbol for Aum. It can be deeply relaxing to draw this mantra, or even listen to the sound of Aum being chanted while you are doing other things.

❋**MALA PRACTICE:** Using a mala, recite the mantra silently or aloud in rounds of 108.

❋**CHANTING PRACTICE:** Using the kirtan recording from the practice companion, sing a mantra along with the digital download track in the call-and-response style.

❋**LISTENING PRACTICE:** Either sitting or walking, open to the sounds all around you. Receptively listen for the sound of **AUM** deep within the everyday sounds you hear. You can close by tuning into the sound of Aum that exists deep within you.

❋**BREATH PRACTICE:** Using the natural rhythm of the breath, silently repeat Aum on every inhale and exhale. This can be done anytime, anywhere, for any length of time.

❋**WALKING PRACTICE:** Walking at a natural pace, silently (or aloud) recite the mantra Aum with each step.

❋**WRITING + DRAWING PRACTICE:** Write out the mantra in Sanskrit or color in the outline of the Sanskrit mantra.

AUM SHANTI

❀ **MANTRA:** Aum Shanti

❀ **PRONUNCIATION:** *ah-OH-mm SHAN-tee*

❀ **BENEFITS:** Peace of mind, ease of heart, serenity, tranquility

❀ **ASSOCIATED DEITY:** None

❀ **MEANING:** Aum peace

❀ **MYTHOLOGY:** In Sanskrit, the word *shanti* means "peace," "calm," "tranquility," or "harmony." In traditional yogic texts, peace is considered to be one of the greatest benefits of regular meditation or yoga practice. However, working with the mantra Aum Shanti specifically and directly invokes an embodied quality of peace. Aum Shanti is often described as the lack of discord or disharmony, especially in the face of challenges. The mantra Aum Shanti deeply calls for peace for all sentient beings everywhere—the whole cosmos—awakening every being's divine right to live with ease of heart.

Application

Aum Shanti invokes a quality of inner peace and calm that translates to an outward harmony and ease. The word *peace* is often used in Western culture to refer to a state that is dependent on external factors to reach. As long as things are precisely the way we want them to be, we can be peaceful and happy. However, this makes peace a very difficult and fleeting state to attain, which is part of why it has become such an undervalued experience in our culture. The beauty of working with this mantra is that it infuses the practitioner with a deep quality of peace that doesn't rely on external factors to access. When we use the mantra *Aum Shanti*, a serene quality of tranquility opens up from within us, radiating out to all aspects of our life.

Peace sometimes has a negative connotation because there is a certain detachment that is often associated with it. It's not uncommon to see a portrayal of the dippy hippie who is totally at peace with the world by way of deep disconnect and delusion. This is the unfortunate shortcut that many take in an attempt to reach a place of serenity: bypassing how we actually feel by checking out and pretending all is well. Walking the path of peace does not mean we are pretending that things are fine when they are not, and it definitely does not mean that we don't feel things when we feel them. Instead, we are seeking a deeper, embodied sense of calm that the mantra evokes within us and that holds our whole experience. This quality can be hard to understand with our minds, especially when dealing with the many challenges and complexities of life, but this mantra opens an internal space in us where we can hold those contradictions and also be at peace. This quality of peace can be the ground from which we can take action and engage fully with life from a place of clarity and calm.

This mantra is often used as a way to close yoga or meditation classes. In this usage, the focus of the mantra is directed toward all sentient beings, ourselves included. This is similar to loving-kindness (*metta*) meditation practice, which offers well wishes for various recipients. This application of the mantra Aum Shanti is a very connecting technique, as it opens us to a recognition that all beings wish to be happy and live in peace, and that the world would be a significantly better place if we could all experience that.

❋ **MALA PRACTICE:** Using a mala, recite the mantra silently or aloud in rounds of 108.

❋ **CHANTING PRACTICE:** Using the kirtan recording from the practice companion, sing the mantra along with the digital download track in the call-and-response style.

❋ **BREATH PRACTICE:** Using the natural rhythm of the breath, silently repeat the mantra on every inhale and exhale.

❋ **WALKING PRACTICE:** Walking at a natural pace, silently (or aloud) recite the mantra as you walk.

❋ **WRITING + DRAWING PRACTICE:** Using the directions from the practice companion, trace or write out the mantra in Sanskrit, or color in the outlined version of the mantra.

लोकाः समस्ताः सुखिनो भवन्तु ॥

LOKAH SAMASTAH SUKHINO BHAVANTU

❁ **MANTRA:** Lokah Samastah Sukhino Bhavantu

❁ **PRONUNCIATION:** *low-KAAH-ha sa-muh-STAH-ha-soo-khee-NO bhah-van-TOO*

❁ **BENEFITS:** World peace

❁ **ASSOCIATED DEITY:** none

❁ **MEANING:** May all beings everywhere be happy and peaceful

❁ **MYTHOLOGY:** This mantra is taken from the final line of the Mangala Mantra, found in the oldest yogic text in Indo-Iranian culture, the Rig V*eda*, dated to approximately 1700–1100 BCE. It is said that there are yogis deep in the mountains of the Himalayas whose sole purpose in life is to pray for the peace of the world. They sit in meditation day and night, reciting mantras like this one, for the liberation of our world from suffering and ignorance.

This mantra is dedicated to the manifestation of worldwide happiness, joy, and freedom from suffering. It is often used as a closing prayer at the end of a period of practice, much as Aum Shanti is used to close a session. The difference between this mantra and Aum Shanti is that this mantra has a distinct focus of invoking peace *for all beings in the world*, whereas Aum Shanti is a less specific peace invocation that can be directed to whatever recipient you choose.

Application

Inherent in any formal practice session, whether it's a mantra, meditation, or yoga practice, is that this is a time for us to let down our guard and open up. We can be ourselves without feeling the pressure to impress anyone, and simply relax into our being. Mantra practice builds upon this by further opening the heart and calming the mind. However, shifting from this open space to transition back into the real world when we finish our practice is not always easy. The Lokah mantra can be a helpful tool to ease this transition when used at the end of a formal practice period. By taking even a few minutes with this mantra at the end of any practice session, the focus of the practice shifts to include others. In doing so, we lay the groundwork for interacting with others with the same tender quality of heart as we are cultivating in our practice.

This mantra can also be a powerful antidote for the moments when we feel overwhelmed by the suffering in the world and don't know what to do about it. The Lokah mantra reconnects and grounds us into our innate desire for peace and harmony all around us. At first glance, it may appear as though this makes us less engaged in the world; however, its effect is quite the opposite. Practicing this mantra infuses the practitioner over time with a quality of connection that fuels greater compassion and caring in action. This doesn't necessarily mean quitting our day job to join the Peace Corps, but it does develop in us a quality of living informed by deep connection and caring for all, becoming the ground from which all our decisions are made.

❀ **MALA PRACTICE:** Using a mala, recite the mantra silently or aloud in rounds of 108.

❀ **CHANTING PRACTICE:** Using the kirtan recording from the practice companion, sing the mantra along with the digital download track in the call-and-response style.

❀ **WALKING PRACTICE:** Walking at a natural pace, silently (or aloud) recite the mantra as you walk.

❀ **WRITING + DRAWING PRACTICE:** Using the directions from the practice companion, trace or write out the mantra in Sanskrit, or color in the outlined version of the mantra.

MANTRAS
FOR
HEALING

लं वं रं यं हं ॐ

BIJA MANTRAS

❀ **MANTRAS:** Lam, Vam, Ram, Yam, Ham, Aum

❀ **PRONUNCIATION:** *lumm, vumm, rumm, yumm, humm, ah-OH-mm*

❀ **BENEFITS:** Balance and energize the physical, emotional and energy bodies

❀ **ASSOCIATED CHAKRA:**

Lam: Muladhara chakra (root chakra)

Vam: Svadhisthana chakra (sacral chakra)

Ram: Manipura chakra (solar plexus chakra)

Yam: Anahata chakra (heart chakra)

Ham: Vishuddha chakra (throat chakra)

Aum: Ajna chakra (third eye chakra)

Aum: Sahasrara chakra (crown chakra)

❀ **MEANING:** Seed mantras

❀ **MYTHOLOGY**: The word *bija* in Sanskrit means "seed." Bija mantras are single-syllable sounds that activate and balance specific energy centers in the body, known as "*chakras.*" The Sanskrit word *chakra* is most often translated as "wheel" or "disk," and is depicted visually as a wheel with spokes. There are seven major chakras in the body (as well as numerous minor chakras), starting at the base of the spine and moving up to the crown of the head. Each major chakra governs specific anatomical systems in the body, subtle energies, as well as related characteristics and emotions. Each bija mantra is associated with one of these seven major chakras. Bija mantras have been used for thousands of years in classical yoga systems and other Eastern traditions as a means of healing the physical, emotional, and subtle bodies. Chanting each mantra balances and energizes each individual chakra, and, in turn, the body as a whole. The vibrational sound of the seed mantra itself stimulates each chakra to reorient it back to a state of balance.

Application

By chanting the bija mantra for each associated chakra, the practitioner awakens and purifies that energy center, increasing vitality, balance, and overall health. This is wonderful to do as a daily practice, to reset your system. Or if you find you have a specific issue in one area of the body, or one aspect of your life, you can tailor this practice to target that specific area. You can learn more about the related behaviors, emotions, and thought patterns that each chakra governs in the *Little Bit of Chakras*[1] book in this series. There are other bija mantras for particular deities and healing practices if you find yourself drawn this this particular type of mantra practice.

Bija Mantra Practice

Starting at the base of the spine, bring your attention to the first chakra. With all your awareness gathered in that location in the body, chant the mantra Lam seven times, directing the mantra into this region of the body. Repeat two more sets of seven, for a total of three rounds of Lam.

Next, bring your attention to your lower abdomen, close to the spine. With all your awareness gathered in the lower abdomen, chant the mantra Vam seven times, directing the mantra into this region of the body. Repeat two more sets of seven, for a total of three rounds of Vam.

Next, bring your attention to the solar plexus area of the body, close to the spinal column. With all your awareness gathered in the solar plexus, chant the mantra Ram seven times, directing the mantra into this region of the body. Repeat two more sets of seven, for a total of three rounds of Ram.

Next, bring your attention to the center of the chest. With all your awareness gathered in the chest, chant the mantra Yam seven times, directing the mantra into this region of the body. Repeat two more sets of seven, for a total of three rounds of Yam.

Next, bring your attention to throat area. With all your awareness gathered in the throat, chant the mantra Ham seven times, directing the mantra into this region of the body. Repeat two more sets of seven, for a total of three rounds of Ham.

Next, bring your attention to the space behind the forehead, in the center of the brain. With all your awareness gathered in the space behind the forehead, chant the mantra Aum seven times, directing the mantra into this region of the body. Repeat two more sets of seven, for a total of three rounds of Aum.

Now bring your attention to the top of the head. With all your awareness gathered in the crown area, chant the mantra Aum once, loud and long, directing the mantra into this region of the body. Repeat two more single sets, for a total of three rounds of Aum.

This practice can also be done by silently repeating the mantras.

SOHAM

❀ **MANTRA:** Soham

❀ **PRONUNCIATION:** *so-HUM*

❀ **BENEFITS:** Expansion and connection

❀ **ASSOCIATED DEITY**: None

❀ **MEANING:** I am that, I am the divine

❀ **MYTHOLOGY**: This mantra can be found in a number of yogic texts, including one the primary vedic texts, the *Mukhya Upanishads. Soham* means "I am that," which is traditionally thought to mean "I am that which is divine." This is like recognizing that the same spark of divine creation suffuses our own being, just as it does the rest of the universe. Instead of only identifying with ourselves as a limited physical body, we instead expand our sense of self to identify as something more infinite: a cosmic self, the "ultimate reality."[2] This makes this mantra an extremely connective and expansive practice.

This mantra is also found in the related form: *Hamsa*. This variation of the mantra is translated as "that I am," yielding a slightly different nuance meaning than "I am that." Soham has the energetic feeling of moving from oneself to expand out and connect to everything, whereas

Hamsa is the reverse of that energetic movement, instead drawing everything into our individual being from that with is all around us.

This particular mantra is often connected to the inhale and exhale of the breath in practice. It is traditionally thought that you can hear the sound of this mantra inherently within the natural breath. The sound of *so* is connected to the inhalation and the *ham* is connected to the exhalation. This can be done with a controlled, measured breath count, or simply by following the natural breath cycle with the internal recitation of the mantra while focused on the inhale and exhale.

Application

The vibe of this mantra is all about connection and expansion. Many years ago I would do this mantra while walking the streets of New York City, breathing the city with my whole being. It was especially powerful for me when I was feeling alone, isolated, or disconnected. This mantra shifts perspective from a limited sense of self to a broader perspective, prompting you to feel like you're truly part of something. This mantra reminds us that we are all woven into the same fabric of life, and part of something larger than just ourselves.

The inhalation of *so* is like tapping into the big sense of I, the cosmic spark that vibrates our being, our essential spark. The exhalation of *ham* is like releasing out to connect this feeling to that same spark in all beings everywhere, all of the cosmos. The rhythm of Soham is like the cosmic inhale and exhale that is always ebbing and flowing beneath us, and repeating the mantra is a way to tap into this sensibility.

❀ **MALA PRACTICE:** Using a mala, recite the mantra silently or aloud in rounds of 108.

❀ **CHANTING PRACTICE:** Using the kirtan recording from the practice companion, sing the mantra along with the digital download track in the call-and-response style.

❀ **BREATH PRACTICE:** Using the natural rhythm of the breath, silently repeat so during the inhalation and *ham* during the exhalation.

❀ **WALKING PRACTICE:** Walking at a natural pace, silently (or aloud) recite the mantra as you walk.

❀ **WRITING + DRAWING PRACTICE:** Using the directions from the practice companion, trace or write out the mantra in Sanskrit, or color in the outlined version of the mantra.

7

MANTRAS
FOR
CLARITY

ॐ भूर्भुवः स्वः ।
तत्सवितुर्वरेण्यं
भर्गो देवस्य धीमहि ।
धियो यो नः प्रचोदयात् ॥

GAYATRI MANTRA

❀ **MANTRA:**

Gayatri Mantra

Aum Bhuur-Bhuvah Svah

Tat-Savitur-Varennyam, Bhargo Devasya Dhiimahi

Dhiyo Yo Nah Pracodayaat

❀ **PRONUNCIATION:** *AH-OH-MM BHOOR BHU-WAH SWA-HA,*
TAT SAVI-tur va RENI-yam, bhar-GO DEVA-sya
DHEEM-a-hi, dhiYO YO nuh pra-CHO-day-AT

❀ **BENEFITS:** Wisdom, insight, illumination

❀ **ASSOCIATED DEITIES:** The Goddess Gayatri and Savitr the
Sun God

❀ **MEANING:** Aum, Let us meditate on the glory of the light of
the Sun and may it enlighten our minds

❀ **MYTHOLOGY:** The first written record of the Gayatri Mantra
is from one of the earliest Indo-Iranian texts, the *Rig Veda*, dated to
approximately 1700–1100 BCE. There is also mention of this mantra
in several other important Hindu texts, including the *Upanishads* and
the *Bhagavad Gita*. The Sanskrit word *gayatri* refers to the meter,

consisting of twenty-four syllables that this mantra is composed in, known as the "*gayatri meter.*"

The personification of the gayatri mantra is the Gayatri goddess, who is considered to be the mother of the Vedas, the oldest of the Hindu texts and scriptures. Gayatri is a form of Saraswati, who was the wife of Brahma. Gayatri is also viewed as the female form of the light of the sun, Savitr. The embodiment of light, wisdom, and illumination, she is the patron of artists, musicians, and poets, as well as the goddess of learning. She is depicted with five faces and ten eyes, which look in eight directions plus the direction of the earth and sky. She has ten hands, holding various types of weapons, attributed to Brahma, Vishnu, and Shiva. One of her primary powers is that she can remove obstacles and bring enlightenment and clarity.

Application

This mantra is an invocation, a contemplation, and a celebration of the divine light of the sun in many forms. The first form is the light of the physical sun that keeps our planet alive, growing the food we eat and nourishing our bodies. In practicing this mantra, we offer our praise and gratitude to the sun, and, in so doing, we open to a sensibility of gratitude for the many ways we are supported in our life. The second form of light this mantra speaks to is the inner light that animates all things. Some call this the light of the soul, others the light of God, and still others refer to it as the divine light. In chanting the Gayatri Mantra, we call upon this inner light to illuminate and awaken our consciousness. In traditional Hindu texts, it is said that enlightenment arises from chanting this mantra by purifying the mind, which is a way of describing profound states of understanding, clarity, and radiance of the mind.

The Gayatri Mantra helps to release and soothe anxiety, opening to a more expansive, creative state of mind. This illumination and the subsequent clarity of mind are also related to taking right action in our lives. The Sanskrit word for action, *dharma*, is considered a path of skillful action. So, the additional benefit of this mantra is illumination that leads to skillful action. This can be a wonderful mantra to practice if you are having a hard time making an important decision or are uncertain about what course of action to take.

❀ **MALA PRACTICE:** Using a mala, recite the mantra silently or aloud in rounds of 108.

❀ **CHANTING PRACTICE:** Using the kirtan recording from the practice companion, sing the mantra along with the digital download track in the call-and-response style.

❀ **WALKING PRACTICE:** Walking at a natural pace, silently (or aloud) recite the mantra as you walk.

❀ **WRITING + DRAWING PRACTICE:** Using the directions from the practice companion, trace or write out the mantra in Sanskrit, or color in the outlined version of the mantra.

AUM ASATO MA SADGAMAYA

❁ **MANTRA:**

Aum Asato Ma Sadgamaya

Tamaso Ma Jyotir-Gamaya

Mrtyor-Ma Amrtam Gamaya

Aum Shanti Shanti Shanti

❁ **PRONUNCIATION:** *ah-OH-mm AAH-sah-tow-MAA SAD g ah-mah-yah, TAH-mah-so MAH joe-TEER GAH-MAH-yah, mrit-your-MAH amriT-AHM gah-mah-YAH, ah-OH-mm SHAN-tee SHAN-tee SHANT-tee*

❁ **BENEFITS:** Peace through clear seeing

❁ **ASSOCIATED DEITY:** None

❁ **MEANING:** Aum, lead me from the unreal to the real, lead me from darkness to light, lead me from death to immortality, Aum peace peace peace

❁ **MYTHOLOGY:** This mantra is part of a larger group of mantras, collectively known as the "shanti mantras." They're found in the Hindu texts, the *Upanishads*. According to Hindu tradition, the shanti mantras, or peace mantras, are a collection of mantras that cultivate tranquility across three areas of pain or misery. The first realm pertains to pain caused by other beings, such as other people or animals. The second realm concerns pain caused by fate, like natural disasters. The third realm relates to pain caused our own bodies and minds, such as disease or anxiety. The shanti mantras are used to counteract pain in these three arenas of suffering.

This particular mantra focuses on the transformation of our own perception as a pathway to peace. This is slightly different than most mantras, which tend to focus on a particular quality, like compassion or courage. The first line of this mantra, "Asato Ma Satgamaya," translates to "Lead me from unreal to real," a reference to one of the foundations of Hindu thought—that all human beings contain within them a spark that is eternal and divine, and this is who we truly are. Many of the lineages in Hindu philosophy are different pathways aimed at this singular goal of realizing that we are not only a body or a mind, but also home to an infinite soul.

This mantra calls for us to make a shift in our perception to identify with the deepest part of ourselves, which is eternal and divine (the so-called "real"), instead of the limited sense that we are only a body or a mind (the "unreal"). This change of perception is often referred to as the "realization of the true self" in Eastern traditions, or "self-realization." In this philosophy, when we correctly identify with the soul, many of the root causes of suffering fall away, and we will abide in a deep place of connection and wisdom.

The next lines elucidate this concept even further: "Lead me from darkness to light, lead me from death to immortality." Here the word *darkness* implies ignorance, doubt, or lack of knowledge, and the word *light* refers to wisdom and truth. The third line, about death and immortality, refers again to shifting our identification to the soul, which in Hindu culture is thought to continue existing after death, eventually reincarnating in many lives across time.

Application

In practical application, this mantra is a wonderful catalyst for transformation by helping you gain profound clarity in daily life. By repeating it, you can shift out of the muddy waters of confusion and gain the luminous power of clarity. This is like cleaning off the windshield of your life to access a clearer view of what's really happening. From there we can take appropriate action with greater accuracy because we're not stuck in our own version of what we think is happening, but instead we can see what is actually happening.

Being able to have this kind of clarity can be a huge game-changer when it comes to navigating life with greater proficiency, less fear, and less anxiety. For example, if you are in a meeting with your boss and she is being snappish with you, it's easy to jump to the conclusion that you've done something wrong. However, by consciously moving from unreal to real and clearing off the windshield of your fears or insecurities, you can look again and see with greater clarity. Perhaps she was up all night taking care of a sick child and is just having a bad day that doesn't have anything to do with you. With this clear seeing, you can offer some extra support, instead of responding with defensiveness that might exacerbate the situation.

You can apply this mantra by taking a moment to pause when things in life are muddy, repeat the mantra for a few minutes, and then take another look at your life from the perspective of these questions: "What is really true here? Am I seeing clearly?"

This approach can also be applied more broadly in your life, especially as an effective tool and support system for shifting larger patterns. For example, if you've been stuck in a pattern of toxic relationships, you can work with this mantra as a means to gain clarity as to how and why you are repeating this cycle in your life. You can work with the mantra for a period of time, like a week or a month, directing it to the specific elements of these relationships in the past and present. Slowly, the mantra has a way of opening up your understanding of those situations, giving you a more honest look at all the subtle dynamics at play, and offering clarification. This mantra moves you from darkness to the light, and, in so doing, leads you to greater peace of mind and ease in life.

❋ **MALA PRACTICE:** Using a mala, recite the mantra silently or aloud in rounds of 108.

❋ **CHANTING PRACTICE:** Using the kirtan recording from the practice companion, sing the mantra along with the digital download track in the call-and-response style.

❋ **WALKING PRACTICE:** Walking at a natural pace, silently (or aloud) recite the mantra as you walk.

❋ **WRITING + DRAWING PRACTICE:** Using the directions from the practice companion, trace or write out the mantra in Sanskrit, or color in the outlined version of the mantra.

MANTRAS
FOR
STRENGTH

हरे कृष्ण हरे कृष्ण
कृष्ण कृष्ण हरे हरे
हरे राम हरे राम
राम राम हरे हरे

MAHA MANTRA

❀ **MANTRA:** Hare Krishna Hare Krisha Krishna Krishna Hare Hare
Hare Ram Hare Ram Ram Ram Hare Hare

❀ **PRONUNCIATION:** *HA-re KRISH-nuh HA-re KRISH-nuh*
KRISH-nuh KRISH-nuh HA-re HA-re
HA-re RAAM HA-re RAAM RAAM RAAM HA-re HA-re

❀ **BENEFITS:** Transcendental awareness, self-realization

❀ **ASSOCIATED DEITIES:** Vishnu, in the form of Krishna, and
Radha

❀ **MEANING:** Great mantra

❀ **MYTHOLOGY:** The Sanskrit word *maha* literally means
"great," so the name of this mantra translates to "great mantra." This
considered by many to be the most potent Sanskrit mantra of all.
Maha mantra comprises three different Sanskrit names—*Hare,*
Krishna, and *Ram*—arranged in a specific order and repetition. The
first Sanskrit name, *Hare,* is often translated as Hara, which is a
variant of the Hindu deity, Radha. Radha, an embodiment of the

divine feminine and the consort of Krishna, also symbolizes the soul. The second Sanskrit name in the mantra, Krishna, is one of the main Hindu deities, a form and avatar of Vishnu. The third Sanskrit name, Ram, is one of the other major deities in the Hindu pantheon and is also an avatar of Vishnu.

According to Hindu mythology, Vishnu is one of the three principal deities that together form the *trimurti*, or "three forms," of cosmic function: creation, preservation, and destruction. Brahma, the first of these three, is known as the creator; Vishnu, the second deity, is the sustainer in charge of preservation; and Shiva, the third deity, is the destroyer. As part of Vishnu's role in this divine trinity, he has incarnated on earth as nine different avatars during times of need, in order to restore and preserve the balance of light and darkness in the world. The best-known of these incarnations is Ram in the story of *The Ramayana*, as well as his incarnation as Krishna in the epic tale *The Mahabharata*, and in the *Bhagavad Gita*. In this context, maha mantra is viewed as an invocation (or celebration) of these forms of the deity Vishnu. In other lineages of Hindu mythology, maha mantra is considered to be a celebration of the union and love between Vishnu (in the form of Krishna) and his divine consort, Radha.

Maha Mantra has garnered the most attention of all Sanskrit mantras in pop culture, often associated with the Hare Krishna organization, as well as making appearances in songs by the Beatles, Tenacious D,[3] Alice Coltrane,[4] Boy George,[5] and Allen Ginsberg[6] in the sixties, and more recently in the TV show, *Mad Men*.[7]

"Of all mantras, the Maha Mantra has been prescribed as the easiest and surest way for attaining God Realization in this present age."

—GEORGE HARRISON[8]

Application

Maha Mantra is a potent mantra that has the ability to shift the energy in the body and mind. It transmutes the denser emotional states into lighter ones. Ancient yogic texts say that the practice of chanting or reciting the name of Hare is a path to realizing the true self.

One of the places I first experienced the potent energy of Maha Mantra was during a month-long trip I took to northern India in 2011. There, in Rishikesh, nestled in the hills of the Himalayas, is the Sivandana Ashram. I had heard many stories about a hall in the ashram from Krishna Das over the years. In 1943, this particular hall was consecrated solely for the purpose of chanting Maha Mantra to bring about world peace.[9] In the seventy-plus years since that time, Maha Mantra has been continuously recited in the hall for twenty-four hours a day, seven days a week, without pause. People come from all over India to live out the final months of their lives chanting Maha Mantra for hour-long shifts as a final service to the world before they die. It's a little difficult to describe the feeling when you walk into this hall, but it's as though you were entering another world altogether. There is a density in the air, a palpable quality that pulls you into another space where the mind is quiet and unhurried. Only one other person was in the hall when I entered the room—an elderly man who was half speaking, half singing the mantra in a deep squeaky voice. He wasn't pleasant to listen to by any means, but I found myself transfixed, as though I had moved into a stream of transcendent consciousness, stretching far behind me and far ahead of me. Oftentimes, when I recite Maha Mantra, I imagine that I am reconnecting with that continuous stream of practice far away in the Himalayas, and reconnecting to the transcendent awareness that the mantra unlocks as well.

❋**MALA PRACTICE:** Using a mala, recite the mantra silently or aloud in rounds of 108.

❋**CHANTING PRACTICE:** Using the kirtan recording from the practice companion, sing the mantra along with the digital download track in the call-and-response style.

❋**BREATH PRACTICE:** Using the natural rhythm of the breath, silently repeat, *Hare Krishna Hare Krishna Krishna Krishna Hare Hare* on every inhalation and *Hare Ram Hare Ram Ram Ram Hare Hare* on each exhalation. This can be done anytime, anywhere, for any duration.

❋**WALKING PRACTICE:** Walking at a natural pace, silently (or aloud) recite the mantra as you walk.

❋**WRITING + DRAWING PRACTICE:** Using the directions from the practice companion, trace or write out the mantra in Sanskrit, or color in the outlined version of the mantra.

RAM

- ❀ **MANTRA:** Ram (also spelled Rama)
- ❀ **PRONUNCIATION:** *RAAM-uh*
- ❀ **BENEFITS:** Devotion and courage
- ❀ **ASSOCIATED DEITY:** Rama
- ❀ **MEANING:** The name of the Hindu deity Rama
- ❀ **MYTHOLOGY:** Rama is a Hindu deity primarily known as the heroic protagonist from the epic story *The Ramayana*. The ancient story of the Ramayana is one of the most popular tales in Hindu culture, so common that kids grow up on cartoon versions of the story on TV. It is credited to the Hindu sage Valmiki, and was written in the form of a 24,000-verse poem somewhere between the seventh and the fourth centuries BCE.

The story chronicles a courageous battle between the forces of dark and light, in which Rama restores the balance in the world against a ten-headed demon named Ravana. In the story, the wife of Rama, Sita, is abducted by Ravana and held captive. Rama searches throughout the land trying to find Sita, enlisting the help of a monkey god named Hanuman to find her. Hanuman, another favorite Hindu deity, helps Rama to find Sita by leaping over an ocean and many other remarkable deeds of service. As with much traditional folklore, the story holds deeper teachings, rooted in Hindu philosophy. The themes of the narrative are related to service, ethics, and duty as pathways to liberation. Rama is an avatar of Vishnu in the story, taking form on earth as the embodiment of virtue, goodness, and devotion to his duty in life, his family, and his work. The narrative in *The Ramayana* plays a vital role in modern Hindu culture as a cornerstone of Hindu values and the Hindu way of life.

Application

Ram Dass (aka Richard Alpert) famously popularized the stories of Rama after returning from India in the late 1960s and sharing the teachings of his Indian guru, Neem Karoli Baba (know more commonly as Maharaj-ji). Maharaj-ji was a devotee of Rama and considered him to be both the pathway of practice and the goal of practice. The only formal practice he taught was taking the name of Rama by repeating the mantra Ram. Maharaj-ji said, "The best form in which to worship God is all forms." Ram Dass goes on to explain: "Everyone you meet is Ram who has come to teach you something. Mantra is remembering that place in the heart—Ram, Ram, Ram. Say it, mouth it, think it, feel it in your heart. You are continually meeting and merging into perfection."[10] This gives you a sense of the depth of connection that can be forged with a mantra, or a deity. Repetition of the mantra awakens a deep remembering of the deepest place you know in yourself, and the practice of reciting the mantra offers a pathway to return to that place again and again.

One interesting way to understand this is to view the various Hindu deities and their associated mythology as different expressions of the inner aspects of our being. When I read a story like the Ramayana, each of the characters in the story represents an aspect of myself: the part of me searching for the truth, the part of me sabotaging the truth, the part of me that is the truth, and so on. For me, this has been the most powerful application of the Hindu mythology, especially when trying to understand why I'm drawn to certain stories and deities. In this light, when we repeat the mantra for Rama, we call upon the aspect of ourselves that is wholly dedicated and devoted. We awaken a golden strength in virtue, clarity, and courage to fight for the truth and to right what is wrong in the world. Rama gives us the power to stay connected to the truth, even when we feel far away from it. He shows us how to love what is most important to us, nurturing it to thrive and grow fully. Another well-known Maharaj-ji devotee, Krishna Das, beautifully explains what is uncovered by repeating the Ram mantra, "Maharaj-ji used to always say, 'Ram nam karne se sab pura ho jata.' From repeating these Names, Ram Nam, the Names of God, everything is brought to fullness and completion. The heart is made full, your life is made full, the karmas are completed in full. It's a ripening process."[11]

"Place the name of Rama as a jeweled lamp at the door of your lips and there will be light, as you will, both inside and out."

—THE RAMAYANA, BY TULSIDAS

PRO TIP:
VARIATIONS ON A THEME

When a mantra is the name of a deity,
it's common to find different variations of the mantra.

For example, some common variations of Ram are:

❋ *Shri Ram Jai Ram Jai Jai Ram* (victory to Rama)

❋ *Hare Ram* (another name for Rama)

❋ *Sita Ram* (Sita is the name of Rama's consort)

❋ *Rama Bolo* (praise or sing to Rama)

❋ *Raghupati Raghava Raja Ram* (O Lord Rama, chief of the Raghus)

❋ *Ramachandra* (Ram as gentle as the moon)

Each variation invokes a different
quality of the deity.

  ❋ ❋ ❋

❀ **MALA PRACTICE:** Using a mala, recite the mantra silently or aloud in rounds of 108.

❀ **CHANTING PRACTICE:** Using the kirtan recording from the practice companion, sing the mantra along with the digital download track in the call-and-response style.

❀ **BREATH PRACTICE:** Using the natural rhythm of the breath, silently repeat the mantra on every inhale and exhale.

❀ **WALKING PRACTICE:** Walking at a natural pace, silently (or aloud) recite the mantra as you walk.

❀ **WRITING + DRAWING PRACTICE:** Using the directions from the practice companion, trace or write out the mantra in Sanskrit, or color in the outlined version of the mantra.

जय जगदम्बे मा दुर्गा

JAYA JAGATAMBE MA DURGA

❋ **MANTRA:** Jaya Jagatambe Ma Durga

❋ **PRONUNCIATION:** *JAY-uh ju-guh-TUM-bey MAA DUUR-gaa*

❋ **BENEFITS:** Courage, bravery, fierce compassion

❋ **ASSOCIATED DEITY:** Durga

❋ **MEANING:** Victory to Durga, the mother of the world

❋ **MYTHOLOGY:** The origin story of Durga concerns a heroic battle between good and evil, told in the Hindu text the *Devi Mahatmya*, which dates to 400–600 CE. As the story goes, the shape-shifting demon Mahishasura earned the boon that he could not be defeated by any man, god, or demon, so he freely terrorized the earth, causing great harm to all. One by one, the gods attempted to thwart his evil doings, but were defeated. They feared that darkness and ignorance would triumph. Upon realizing that a woman could possibly defeat this enemy, the gods joined forces to create the fiercest female warrior the world had ever seen. The resulting goddess came to be known as Durga, whose Sanskrit name literally means "impassable" or "invincible"; she was also known as "the one who eliminates suffering." Durga's mount is a tiger or a lion, and she is depicted with eight arms that wield the weapons given to her by Brahma, Vishnu, and Shiva. Once created, Durga battled tirelessly with Mahishasura for nine days, ultimately defeating him and restoring peace and the balance in the world.

Primarily, Durga is celebrated as a tremendous warrior; however, underlying her great fighting prowess is a profound compassion, together with a deep concern for maintaining the goodness of the world. In the depictions of her battle with Mahishasura, her face is described as serene and calm, even in the most harrowing moments, revealing her deep grounding in love and righteousness. Durga can take fierce action to correct some wrongdoing, but without succumbing to fear, hatred, or ignorance. She exemplifies great love and care, while protecting others and doing whatever is necessary to keep them safe. In playing this role, she shows how formidable the qualities of compassion and love can be, like the mother who lifts a car to save her child. In this way, Durga fights to protect those who cannot protect themselves, standing up against oppression, tyranny, and darkness to restore goodness and agency for all.

The Sanskrit word jagatambe is also a name for Durga, literally translated as *"the mother of the world."* This alternate name for Durga is a slightly different way of characterizing her, as the compassionate caregiver and wise protector, likening her more to a mother archetype.

Some of Durga's other forms (Kali, Bhairavi, Ambika) are the most ferocious in the Hindu pantheon, wielding weapons of mass destruction, wearing the skulls of her victims as a necklace, and even licking up their rival's spilled blood. However menacing these forms of Durga seem, they actually represent her unrelenting fearlessness in confronting the worst injustice, staying true to her name as "the one who removes suffering."

Application

One application of the mythology of Durga is to work with her sensibility and energy on the inner landscape of our lives. Calling on Durga with this mantra invokes the capacity within ourselves to face our demons and conquer our greatest fears. The Durga mantra offers us all the tools we need to fight our own battles: firm conviction, positive energy, sharpness of knowledge, freedom from doubt, and fearlessness born of wisdom. These tools, all expressions of Durga's compassion, help us to be more skillful in caring for others and ourselves. She supports us in rewiring unhealthy habits and conditioning that are no longer in alignment with our deepest values. She also helps us confront our inner critic and our inner demons, those negative voices working to convince us that we will never succeed or that will we never be loved. In their place, the Durga invocation fosters an inner environment of warmth and kindness for ourselves, including balanced self-care with an acknowledgment of our basic goodness. Durga helps us feel at home in our own mind and heart by first empowering us with courage, and then gently tending to the aspects of ourselves that need the warmth of unconditional care.

The other application for the Durga mantra is in the field of our life. The world around us is often a complex and demanding place. If we are in a challenging situation and don't know the best course of action, this mantra can help us find the clarity and courage to do what is needed. The energy of Durga also empowers us to set clear boundaries around the things we are not comfortable doing in a given situation. Durga gives us permission to say no when we need to, with the authority to advocate for both ourselves and others when we see injustice. Durga's ability to take strong action can embolden us to do the same, standing in our truth to fight for what we value most in the world. She teaches us how to fiercely love and protect what we hold dearest, whether it be our children, our partners and friends, or our work or artistic undertakings. For some, it means fighting to protect the land we live on and the natural resources that sustain us, while for others it means working for freedom and justice for underserved and oppressed communities. Durga ignites the fire within us to expand how and who we love, offering a pathway to become a true warrior of love.

❈ **MALA PRACTICE:** Using a mala, recite the mantra silently or aloud in rounds of 108.

❈ **CHANTING PRACTICE:** Using the kirtan recording from the practice companion, sing the mantra along with the digital download track in the call-and-response style.

❈ **BREATH PRACTICE:** Using the natural rhythm of the breath, silently repeat the mantra on every inhale and exhale.

❈ **WALKING PRACTICE:** Walking at a natural pace, silently (or aloud) recite the mantra as you walk.

❈ **WRITING + DRAWING PRACTICE:** Using the directions from the practice companion, trace or write out the mantra in Sanskrit, or color in the outlined version of the mantra.

MANTRAS
FOR
LIBERATION

ॐ गं गणपतये नमः ॥

AUM GAM GANAPATAYE NAMAHA

❋ **MANTRA:** Aum Gam Ganapataye Namaha

❋ **PRONUNCIATION:** *ah-OH-mm GUM gun-na-pat-tay-YAE nu-muh-HAH*

❋ **BENEFITS:** Success, prosperity, removal of obstacles

❋ **ASSOCIATED DEITY:** Ganesha

❋ **MEANING:** I bow down to the remover of obstacles, Ganesha

❋ **MYTHOLOGY:** Gam is the seed mantra for the Hindu deity Ganesha. Every deity has his or her own seed mantra, which is like a direct line to call upon that particular deity.

Ganesha, one of the more popular deities in the Hindu pantheon, is universally respected in subcultures of the Hindu tradition. He is known as the elephant god, depicted with the head of an elephant atop a human body. He is typically shown with a protruding belly and four arms, and his mount is a very small mouse. He can be portrayed as sitting, standing, in a yoga pose, crawling like a child, dancing, or even sitting with his mother. Ganesh is thought to be the son of Shiva and his consort Parvati, though there are many different tales explaining how he came into existence.

Primarily, Ganesh is the remover of obstacles, often called on at the beginning of any undertaking to ensure success and completion. He is also considered by Hindus to be in charge of learning and intelligence, and, by invoking him, we increase the chances for success and prosperity in all our endeavors.

One of the delightful characteristics of Ganesh is his giant Buddha belly. His belly is thought to represent the space of the universe—the past, the present, and the future. In one story it is said that Ganesh draws all the suffering of the world into his belly to transmute it for the good of all beings everywhere.

Application

This mantra is great to recite when we are feeling stuck or blocked. When we encounter an obstacle in life, we may not feel super-creative in response to the obstacle facing us. More likely, we get frustrated or annoyed that things are not going according to plan. Ganesh has a way of helping us to approach these inevitable moments with more spaciousness and curiosity. There are many ways to remove an obstacle: We can shift our approach, we can open a dialogue, we can let go of the way we think it's supposed to come together, or we can wait with patience for better timing. Invoking Ganesh helps us to see the different possibilities in what can otherwise be a time of narrow vision and fearfulness. This mantra helps us get to the finish line with greater ease and joy.

This mantra also helps us to reconnect to our desires and figure out how to best bring them to life. Meeting an obstacle en route to any goal or destination in life forces us to reconnect and recommit to where we're going. Even if it's something as simple as roadwork on your daily commute, if the roadwork is bad enough, you might just turn around and go home. But if you love your job so much that you really, really want to get there, you will reconnect to that desire and figure out another way to get there, even if it means taking a hot-air balloon! Life is often not a straight shot, and in order to reach our goals, we have to be savvy, creative, and resourceful. Working with this Ganesh mantra is a wonderful way to cultivate that sensibility.

❀ **MALA PRACTICE:** Using a mala, recite the mantra silently or aloud in rounds of 108.

❀ **CHANTING PRACTICE:** Using the kirtan recording from the practice companion, sing the mantra along with the digital download track in the call-and-response style.

❀ **WALKING PRACTICE:** Walking at a natural pace, silently (or aloud) recite the mantra as you walk.

❀ **WRITING + DRAWING PRACTICE:** Using the directions from the practice companion, trace or write out the mantra in Sanskrit, or color in the outlined version of the mantra.

AUM NAMAH SHIVAYA

❊ **MANTRA:** Aum Namah Shivaya

❊ **PRONUNCIATION:** *ah–OH–mm nuh–MAA shee–VIE–yuh*

❊ **BENEFITS:** Release and transformation

❊ **ASSOCIATED DEITY:** Shiva

❊ **MEANING:** I bow to the inner self, I bow to the auspicious one, I bow to the true self.

❊ **MYTHOLOGY:** In Hindu mythology, the concept of the cosmos is personified by a trio of deities that represent the cycle of birth, life, and death. These three deities are the most significant gods in the Hindu pantheon and, together, are called the *trimurti*, or "three forms," of cosmic function: creation, preservation, and destruction. Brahma is known as the creator, Vishnu as the sustainer, and Shiva as the destroyer. In this mythology, Shiva the "destroyer" is sometimes referred to as the "transformer." Stories of Shiva abound in yogic texts dating back thousands of years. He is viewed as a great yogi, practicing meditation for thousands of years at a time, and living a life of austere renunciation. It is said that Shiva oversees the endings and changing of cycles in the cosmos, guiding us through death and transformation.

The mantra Aum Namah Shivaya translates from Sanskrit to "I bow to Shiva" or "I bow to the true self," as Shiva is classically thought to represent the true self that is left after everything else ends—the timeless and immortal witness. There are many Shiva devotees in India and beyond, known in India as Shaivites, many of whom are yogis and wandering monks. They immerse themselves in the practices and rituals of Shiva. This mantra is traditionally used in these lineages, and it is believed that the wholehearted undertaking of this mantra can purify the mind so that one can become fully enlightened. This, in part, is because Shiva is thought to govern not only destruction in the outer world, but also destruction in the inner realms. He is considered to be the destroyer of the ego; by invoking him with this mantra, the ardent practitioner can merge entirely with the cosmic consciousness. In northern India, in the foothills of the Himalayas, it's common to see wandering monks mumbling this mantra under their breath.

Application

This mantra offers an embodied understanding of the value and importance of the dissolution of things, whether on a major or a minor level. Western culture places a monumental emphasis on accumulating things: money, success, clothes, friends, hobbies. The underlying message in every ad is that the more we acquire, the happier we will be. But we've all seen firsthand examples of people with immense success who are utterly miserable. And the truth is that all things come and go—whether it's something we love deeply or something have a great aversion to. That is the very cycle of life. Aum Namah Shivaya helps to bring about an embodied sense of this larger perspective, helping us to loosen the death grip we often have on the thing we cherish most. In practical terms this allows us to be more in the flow of life and less fearful about the changes that lie ahead. We can gracefully let go, with gratitude and a full heart. This mantra supports us when cleaning out our closet to create space in our life, letting go of old habits that no longer serve us, or grieving the loss of a cherished pet. It allows us to be more in harmony with the natural cycles of life, understanding the bigger picture that when all things begin, they will eventually end; in so doing, we can cherish the time that we do have with anyone or anything. We are all faced with loss of some kind in our lives; it is the one thing we can be certain of. Working with this mantra can help train us to be able to walk through those times with spaciousness, curiosity, and wisdom.

This mantra also helps us overcome the fear of death, as it brings us an understanding that is grounded in a deep grasp of the nature of reality: everything that comes into form will eventually lose that form. Recognizing this core truth makes life especially poignant and help us to cherish the time we do have with less fear. Instead of getting caught up in the stuff that fills or lives, or the thoughts that fill our minds, we can place our place our faith in a deeper sense of self. By chanting this mantra, we invoke Shiva and, in so doing, call on the aspect of ourselves that has the capacity to let go with ease, that is timeless, and that knows no bounds—the innermost part of ourselves that sits, unwavering, like a mountain, even in the most

tumultuous times. This mantra offers great peace of mind, connecting us to our deeper sense of self.

❀ **MALA PRACTICE:** Using a mala, recite the mantra silently
or aloud in rounds of 108.

❀ **CHANTING PRACTICE**: Using the kirtan recording from
the practice companion, sing the mantra along with the
digital download track in the call-and-response style.

❀ **BREATH PRACTICE:** Using the natural rhythm of the
breath, silently repeat the mantra on every inhale and exhale.

❀ **WALKING PRACTICE**: Walking at a natural pace, silently
(or aloud) recite the mantra *Aum Namah Shivaya* with
each step.

❀ **WRITING + DRAWING PRACTICE:** Using the directions
from the practice companion, trace or write out the mantra
in Sanskrit, or color in the outlined version of the mantra.

जय गुरुदेव

JAI GURUDEV

- ❈ **MANTRA**: Jai Gurudev
- ❈ **PRONUNCIATION**: *JAAY gu-ru-DEV*
- ❈ **BENEFITS:** Wisdom, clarity, humility
- ❈ **ASSOCIATED DEITY:** Guru or teacher (inner and outer)
- ❈ **MEANING**: Victory to the teacher within me, the one that knows
- ❈ **MYTHOLOGY:** *Jai Gurudev* is a mantra related to the guru.

The Sanskrit word *guru* can be broken down to two aspects: *Gu* literally means "darkness," and *ru* means "light." Combined, the word means "from darkness to light" or "the remover of darkness." In the more esoteric translations of the word, it is thought that the guru is the most indwelling, all-knowing aspect of ourselves— the part of us that is fully illuminated, fully enlightened, free from ignorance, the part of us who knows. In traditional Hindu thought, when we encounter a teacher in our lives, he is actually just a reflection of this inner guru and teacher. The outer teacher is reflecting back to us the wisdom already within us, and merely helps us to fully realize and uncover our own innate wisdom. In chanting the mantra Jai Gurudev, we call for the victory of the guru within our own hearts and minds. We call for the removal of

A LITTLE BIT OF MANTRAS

ignorance in our own being. This mantra is an invocation of the teacher within us to illuminate a pathway to our deepest wisdom and happiness.

In the East, the guru is considered to be the embodiment of the finest virtues of being human. The guru is also the teacher who passes along the techniques and philosophy of a spiritual lineage for others to learn from and adopt. Gurus empower students or seekers on their individual path of discovery, in whatever form that may take. In the Hindu tradition, a family guru may serve a role similar to that of a wise grandfather or grandmother in the family unit. The guru's advice is sought for simple household matters like which job to take or how to handle a difficult family situation.

Sadly, the concept and tradition of the guru has been terribly abused, distorted, and corrupted by many, and is one of the hardest concepts to translate from Eastern to Western culture. The role of guru is so foreign to Western culture that it's led to some bizarre and harmful incarnations. Examples abound of people claiming to be gurus, who are actually just exploiting others or using their position to oppress others and acquire power under the pretext of "helping others." So it's good to understand that this mantra is not at all about giving away your power; rather, it's about helping you to reclaim it. We don't have to rely on someone else in our life to learn, grow, and move forward, and this mantra can act as a catalyst to do just that. We can figure out for ourselves what we need to do and how to do it in a healthy way.

Application

This mantra is wonderful during times of confusion and doubt. It has a way of cutting through the clouds of uncertainty to help you find inner clarity and develop the resolve to move forward. This mantra can be a valuable resource and tool for empowerment, helping to cultivate trust in yourself, your instincts, and your gut feeling to deeply inform your life. It's like being able to make a phone call to the future version of yourself who knows the best way forward and what potholes to avoid.

This invocation also cultivates humility. By calling on the part of us that knows, we implicitly acknowledge our not-knowing. We first must empty our cup in order to fill it. So there is some surrender involved when we call on the inner guru—it is a humble call for support when we need it.

Messages from a guru may also come in fun, unconventional forms. It may be a wise insight from a friend, a random scrawl that speaks to us from some passing graffiti on a train, the perfect song that plays when we are listening to music. In working with this mantra, we can open to the wisdom that the universe offers us, especially when we need it most.

❊ **MALA PRACTICE:** Using a mala, recite the mantra silently or aloud in rounds of 108.

❊ **CHANTING PRACTICE:** Using the kirtan recording from the practice companion, sing the mantra along with the digital download track in the call-and-response style.

❊ **BREATH PRACTICE:** Using the natural rhythm of the breath, silently repeat the mantra on every inhale and exhale.

❊ **WALKING PRACTICE:** Walking at a natural pace, silently (or aloud) recite the mantra as you walk.

❊ **WRITING + DRAWING PRACTICE:** Using the directions from the practice companion, trace or write out the mantra in Sanskrit, or color in the outlined version of the mantra.

❖ 10 ❖

DAILY MANTRA APPLICATION

THERE ARE ENDLESS WAYS TO APPLY MANTRA practice to your life beyond the formal practices laid out in earlier in this book. These more informal mantra practices serve as a bridge between the deeper states of being that we access in formal practice and the space we inhabit the rest of the day. By returning to mantras throughout the day, we gently break up the flow of a day in which we may otherwise be running on autopilot. Some of the methods in this chapter are from the Hindu tradition, while others are my own personal application of mantra practice from the past twenty years. These techniques are not meant to be a substitute for formal practice, but rather an extension of them. When integrated fully into your life, they can illuminate your life with intention, focus, and deep connection.

ILLUMINATE THE ROUTINE

One of the simplest ways to bring more mantra practice into your life is by incorporating mantras into daily tasks. Any activity can be a prompt for you to recite a mantra, bringing new meaning to an otherwise ordinary task by giving you the chance to reconnect to your practice and yourself in that moment. This can be as simple as reciting a mantra every time you pass through a doorway or when you hear a notification on your phone. The activity you are choosing to trigger your mantra repetition can be one that happens once a day or many times throughout the day. Depending on what activity you choose, and what mantra you're working with, this can be a single mantra repetition or several repetitions of the mantra. To try this type of informal practice, choose one or two activities for a few days to see how it works for you. Then if it's the right fit for you, you can commit to doing it for a longer period of time. You'll see that it doesn't take long to create the habit to recite the mantra. Here are some common tasks that work well to cue mantra practice:

❀ **Household chores:** Doing dishes, laundry, or other housework.

❀ **Personal hygiene:** Showering, brushing your teeth, washing your face, putting on makeup.

❀ **Traveling:** Play some kirtan recording while driving, walking, biking, taking the subway, or riding the bus.

❀ **Waiting:** When you find yourself waiting at a traffic light or for a meeting to start, or you're in line at the post office.

❀ **Exercise:** Silent mantra practice is a great addition to any form of exercise, whether it's running, swimming, lifting at the gym, yoga class, or skiing. You can even use the mantra as a counting mechanism for how long to hold a position or for marking repetitions.

Some smaller, repeated actions that also work well to cue informal mantra practice include:

❀ Each time you check or use a device

❀ Every time you drink water

❀ Each time you start your car

❀ Every time you open the refrigerator

❀ Every time you wash your hands

❀ Every time you turn on a light

❀ Each time you pass through a doorway

❀ Anytime you greet someone

❀ Every time you send an email

INFORMAL MANTRA PRACTICE

Overcoming Negative Thoughts

Mantras can be an effective tool for working with negative thoughts. In the yogic tradition, this technique is a variation of *Pratipaksha Bhavana*. *Pratipaksha Bhavana* is a practice of working with negative thoughts by consciously thinking the opposite of the thought as a response to it. The mantra variation of this practice is to repeat a mantra whenever you notice a negative thought crossing your mind.

This isn't an attempt to repress or push away the negative thought; instead, it's simply a way to shift your focus elsewhere. This can be implemented whenever you notice the negative thought: Simply follow it by silently repeating the mantra, as though you were capping the thought with the mantra itself. For example, when you notice a thought like "I really sounded dumb in that meeting," you cap the thought with "Aum Namah Shivaya" right afterward. This technique prevents you from going down the wormhole of negative self-talk, simply by shifting your attention elsewhere. So instead of believing that the negative thought is correct, or beating yourself up for even having it in the first place, you can disrupt the process altogether by shifting over to the mantra.

Counteracting Negative Emotions

Mantras can be a powerful antidote to distressing emotional states, like anxiety, fear, or loneliness. If you find yourself struggling in this way, try internally repeating a mantra for a few minutes. A slightly stronger variation of this practice involves synchronizing the silent mantra repetition to the breath. This variation works best with shorter mantras, where you can sync the duration of one repetition to the inhale, and then the next repetition to the exhale. This is a simple way to counteract any physiological flight-or-fight response you may be experiencing as a result of your state of mind.

Empowering Yourself with Protection and Support

In many of the mythic tales of good and evil in Hindu mythology, mantras are used as a form of protection on the battlefield. We can apply that same logic when going into difficult situations by using a mantra to empower ourselves. If you're heading into a situation that you know will be challenging for you, take a few minutes beforehand to charge yourself up with a mantra. You can listen to your favorite kirtan recording, do a few rounds of japa, or write out a mantra to center yourself and bolster your confidence. By taking a few minutes to reconnect with deeper yourself, you can approach the situation in a balanced state of relaxed alertness, instead of coming from a place of fear.

Infusing Food with Positive Energy

Another arena where mantras are regularly used in Indian culture is in the kitchen. It's common in ashrams and temples for mantras to be chanted by those preparing food as a way to infuse the food with positive energy. You can apply the same concept in your own kitchen, doing mantra practice while you are cooking or by chanting a mantra into a dish just before you eat it. In both instances, the purpose is to send the mantra directly into the food itself, charging up the food with positive energy generated by the mantras. Mantra-infused food is thought to be highly beneficial for the person who consumes it, and can be a wonderful healing agent for anyone who is unwell. Beverages can also be charged up with a mantra before being consumed!

Tactile Reminders

Pocket stones or worry stones can be a wonderful tool to handle challenging situations throughout the day, and a mala bracelet or necklace can serve the same purpose. The tactile experience of touching the mala beads can act as a gentle reminder and grounding while you are in a meeting or on the go. And if you have a few minutes to fully concentrate, you can fit in a round of formal mantra practice sprinkled throughout your day.

Mantra Practice for Others

Mantra practice can be done for the benefit of other individuals or groups, especially those who don't have the capacity to practice themselves. If you have a friend who is undergoing surgery, or you know someone going through a tough time, dedicating your mantra practice can be a powerful way to connect to him and send him positive energy and care. Many wandering monks in the Eastern traditions recite mantras solely for the benefit of others. And whether or not you believe in the power of prayer, offering a mantra for those who are suffering can be the genuine gesture of the kindness from the heart.

Mantra practice can also have a wonderful effect on those in close proximity to you, as you chant or speak a mantra aloud for others to hear. Many children love to listen to mantras, as do many animals. The sounds can be soothing to hear, especially when they are having a difficult time. Some parents will play or sing mantras into the womb during pregnancy so that the child will have an auditory anchor after birth.

PRO TIP:
MANTRA KIDS

Many children love to sing, and chanting
mantras can be a wonderful activity to do
together. This can be either a quiet, calming
activity, when needed, or a higher-energy activity
that inspires them to move, dance, or play.

❈ ❈ ❈

DAY OF MANTRA

ON WAKING UP: Aum three times

BREAKFAST: Charge your food with mantra

MORNING PRACTICE: Bija mantras to reset your chakras

COMMUTE TO WORK: Chant in the car or on the subway

WHILE AT WORK: Keep a mala in your pocket and do a round of the following as needed:

> ❁ Before an important meeting: *Aum Gam Ganapataye Namaha*
>
> ❁ Before giving an important speech: *Asato Ma Satgamaya*
>
> ❁ Dealing with a struggling coworker: *Jaya Jagatambe MaDurga*
>
> ❁ When you need mental focus and illumination: *Gayatri Mantra*
>
> ❁ Handling a conflict: *Lokah Samastah*

AT LUNCH: Charge your food with mantra

AFTER LUNCH WALKING PRACTICE: *Soham* five minutes

COMMUTE HOME FROM WORK: Chant in the car, on the subway or the bus

PREPARING DINNER: Charge your food with mantra

FAMILY TIME: Draw or color mantras

PRE-BEDTIME/CLOSE OF THE DAY: *Aum Shanti* three times

As you deepen your relationship to mantra practice, you will find endless ways to bring the practice into your life. You can begin to rely on your practice to support the quality of life that you desire, and tailor it to suit the changing ebb and flow of your life as it unfolds. In challenging times, you can use the practice to gain clarity and courage; in times of quiet, you can unpack your latent creative power; in times of scarcity, you can recharge and create inner space; in times of pain, you can heal and soothe yourself; in times of unrest, you can ground yourself; and in times of joy, you can call forth gratitude in abundance. Have fun with this endless resource!

QUESTIONS ABOUT MANTRAS

❖ **DO I HAVE TO BE A GOOD SINGER TO PRACTICE KIRTAN?** Definitely not! You do not have to be Céline Dion to practice mantra. Some of the most proficient mantra practitioners I know are not musicians—they have gravelly voices, but sing the mantras so wholeheartedly that it's incredibly beautiful to listen to. Remember, this isn't a performance and it's not a competition for who can sing a mantra the perfect way. So while it's important to spend some time learning the pronunciation of a mantra, beyond that, you can let go of any concerns about how you sound in your practice, and just go for it!

❖ **I DON'T FEEL ANYTHING WHEN I DO MANTRA PRACTICE. AM I DOING IT WRONG?** Definitely not! There will be times in your practice that you feel totally peaceful and zen, while moments will feel bored and dry, like nothing is happening. And of course, there will be plenty of days that you are angry, sad or disconnected. All of this is very normal, and it's important to understand that these different emotional states are not reflective of your abilities as a mantra practitioner. Emotions come and go, and are not in our control. It's common to assume that if we feel good in a mantra session, that it's because we're doing something right, and if we feel bad in a mantra session, it's because we're doing something wrong. Don't believe the hype! The real power of this practice is in the cultivation of deeper skills (concentration, resilience, and kindness) below the surface. In other words, mantra practice is not about manufacturing a specific emotional state, but instead discovering new ways to relate to how we feel. Of course, you may choose to work with a mantra to invoke a specific quality in your life, but this is something that emerges naturally over time and not in the same exact practice session. So, a more accurate measure of whether or not you are understanding the spirit of the practice might be: Can I be gentle with myself on days that I'm having a hard time? Can I draw on deeper focus on days that I'm extra scattered? Can I be patience with myself on days that the practice is boring? Can I be tender and let go without judging myself for feeling afraid?

❈ **HOW CAN I TELL IF THE PRACTICE IS WORKING?** To see if the practice is benefiting you, I would recommend first giving yourself a period of time, like a month, to do the practice on a regular basis without constantly assessing it. Once you've put in the time, the best way to assess if the practice is to look at your life, not at the practice itself. Has your general mood shifted since undertaking the practice? If you used lose your temper ten times a month, then it's a definite improvement to only lose it five times now. Another good sign that the practice is working is that you won't stay stuck in the anger for as long as you used to. In other words, you'll still get mad but instead of taking a day to get over it, maybe it only takes you a few hours. Another place to measure whether or not the practice is working is how connected you feel—to yourself and to others. Are you more in tune with your own ebb and flow throughout the day? One final place to check out is how resilient you are. If you encounter a failure or misstep of some kind, are you able to recover more easily than you used to? You can find out for yourself if the practices are helping you enough to warrant continuing with them!

❊ **ARE SOME MANTRA TECHNIQUES BETTER THAN OTHERS?** I recommend finding the technique that you enjoy the most! From a practical point of view, the technique you like most is the one you will do the most, and this is what will benefit you the most. By tailoring your mantra practice to fit your life, you will have greater success with it.

❊ **DO I HAVE TO BE HINDU TO USE MANTRAS?** While these practices come from the Hindu tradition, you don't have to subscribe to the religious practices of that culture to benefit immensely from them. Whatever your faith tradition, mantras can be a tool for you to connect more deeply with those beliefs and values.

❊ **I'VE HEARD THAT YOUR MANTRA SHOULD BE A SECRET. IS THAT TRUE?** There are some traditions that use secret mantras, but most mantras are widely shared.

CONCLUSION

Over the past decade, I have put the practices of sacred sounds to the test, to find out if they can be a force of healing and illumination in my life. I have used mantras during times of immense joy, times of great fear and loss, and all the spaces between. Do the same experiment. Find out for yourself if mantras can really change your life. Put into practice the tools from this book and see what happens. Let your life become a laboratory to discover new ways of being through the power of sacred sounds. I hope they will bring you tremendous peace, clarity, and joy, as they have done for me. राम राम

RESOURCES

Practice Companion

To support your mantra practice, download the free practice companion at www.lilycushman.com/LBOMdownload that includes the following elements for each mantra from the book:

1. Audio Pronunciation Guide
2. Kirtan Recordings for Call-and-Response Singing
3. Writing Mantra Directions
4. Mantra Tracing Guide
5. Mantra Outline for Coloring

Spotify Playlist

Kirtan Playlist by Lily: www.bit.ly/LBOMplaylist

Recommended Kirtan Artists

AMBIKA: ambikachant.com

DEVADAS: devadasmusic.com

JAI UTTAL: jaiuttal.com

KRISHNA DAS: krishnadas.com

NINA RAO: ninaraochant.com

SHYAMA CHAPIN: shyamachapin.com

Mantra Related Sites

BE HERE NOW NETWORK: beherenownetwork.com

CALL AND RESPONSE FOUNDATION: callandresponsefoundation.org

CHARLIE COX MANTRA CALLIGRAPHY: instagram.com/charlie_r_cox

KESHAV MUSIC IMPORTS: keshav-music.com

KIRTAN CENTRAL: kirtancentral.com

MANTRALOGY: mantralogy.com

SANSKRIT STUDIES WITH MANORAMA: sanskritstudies.org

VANARAS MUSIC: vanarasmusic.com

Recommended Reading

Bryant, Edwin F. *Bhakti Yoga: Tales and Teachings from the Bhagavata Purana.* New York: North Point Press, 2017.

Das, Krishna. *Chants of a Lifetime: Searching for a Heart of Gold.* Carlsbad: Hay House, 2010.

Hersey, Baird. *The Practice of Nada Yoga: Meditation on the Inner Sacred Sound.* Rochester: Inner Traditions, 2014.

Kempton, Sally. *Awakening Shakti: The Transformative Power of the Goddesses of Yoga.* Boulder: Sounds True, Inc., 2013.

Rajagopalachari, C., translator. *Mahabharata.* Mumbai, India: Bharatiya Vidya Bhavan, 1951.

———, *translator, Ramayana.* Mumbai, India: Bharatiya Vidya Bhavan, 1951.

Vivekananda, Swami. *Bhakti Yoga: The Yoga of Love and Devotion.* Kolkata, India: Vedanta Press & Bookshop, 1978.

END NOTES

Chapter 1: What Are Mantras?: The History of Sacred Sounds

1. https://en.oxforddictionaries.com/definition/mantra.

2. Jan Westerhoff, *Nagarjuna's Madhyamaka: A Philosophical Introduction* (New York: Oxford University Press, 2009), p. 290.

3. Deepak Sharma, *Classical Indian Philosophy: A Reader* (New York: Columbia University Press, 2011), pp. 196–197.

Chapter 2: The Benefits of Mantra: What Science Says

1. https://www.ncbi.nlm.nih.gov/pubmed/28119651.

2. https://www.liebertpub.com/doi/10.1089/acm.2017.0053.

3. https://www2.le.ac.uk/projects/vgec/highereducation/epigenetics_ethics/Introduction.

4. http://www.orthodoxchristianity.net/forum/index.php?topic=15834.0.

5. https://www.ncbi.nlm.nih.gov/pmc/articles.

6. https://www.ncbi.nlm.nih.gov/pubmed/29752573.

7. Jessica R. Andrews-Hanna, "The Brain's Default Network and Its Adaptive Role in Internal Mentation," *The Neuroscientist: A Review*

Journal Bringing Neurobiology, Neurology and Psychiatry 18, no. 3 (June 1, 2012): 251–270, doi:10.1177/1073858411403316.

8. https://link.springer.com/article/10.1007/s41465-017-0028-1.

9. https://centerhealthyminds.org/news/meditation-expertise-changes-experience-of-pain.

10. https://www.researchgate.net/publication/312383052_A_randomized_controlled_trial_of_Kundalini_yoga_in_mild_cognitive_impairment.

Chapter 4: Formal Mantra Methods

1. Vaman Shivram Apte, *The Practical Sanskrit Dictionary*, p. 447.

2. http://krishnadas.com/lyrics/baba-hanuman/.

Chapter 5: Mantras for Peace

1. Shirley Telles, R. Nagarantha, and H. R. Nagendra, "Autonomic Changes During 'OM' Meditation," *Indian Journal of Physiological Pharmacology 39* (1995): 418–420. https://www.ncbi.nlm.nih.gov/pubmed/8582759.

Chapter 6: Mantras for Healing

1. Mercee, Amy Leigh, *A Little Bit of Chakras: An Introduction to Energy Healing* (New York: Sterling Publishing Co., 2016).

2. Patrick Olivelle, *Samnyasa Upanisads: Hindu Scriptures on Asceticism and Renunciation* (New York, Oxford University Press, 1992), pp. 210.

Chapter 8: Mantras for Strength

1. http://www.iskcon.org/.

2. https://en.wikipedia.org/wiki/My_Sweet_Lord.

3. https://www.youtube.com/watch?v=AQgbYOj4enM.

4. https://www.allmusic.com/song/hare-krishna-mt0000088669.

5. https://en.wikipedia.org/wiki/Jesus_Loves_You_(band).

6. https://www.youtube.com/watch?v=eV5I09j49v8.

7. https://www.youtube.com/watch?v=eygszIuBedQ.

8. "A mantra is mystical energy . . ." George Harrison, *I, Me and Mine* (San Francisco: Chronicle Books, 2002).

9. http://astrologer-astrology.com/ashrams_in_rishikesh.htm.

10. https://www.ramdass.org/mantras-2/.

11. https://www.facebook.com/KrishnaDasMusic/posts/maharaj-ji-used-to-always-say-ram-nam-karne-se-sab-pura-ho-jata-from-repeating-t/10155481385221879/.

ACKNOWLEDGMENTS

First and foremost, I would like to thank my teachers, without whom I would have been long lost, broken, and drowned: Lelelewa, who set me on a path when I was eighteen years old. Dharma Mittra, my first teacher, who first taught me I was capable of so much more than I ever realized, and the many forms that devotion can take. Krishna Das, who brought me home to Maharaj-ji, Siddhi Ma, and my community, and whose care and support I will never be able to fully understand or repay. Sharon Salzberg, who taught me how to love myself and be myself—and cut a path for me to follow. I'm deeply grateful to the staff and teachers at Brooklyn Yoga School over the past nine years. Without your generosity, hard work, and belief in my mission, BYS would never have come to life to help so many. I'm also incredibly grateful to our community of students for continually showing up and doing the work.

I have been graced with the friendship of three great women: Ambika Pressman, Janaki Kagel, and Katurah Hutcheson, who have brought me through my darkest hours, made me laugh until I peed, and without whom I would be utterly lost. Immense gratitude to the talented musicians who have supported my chanting for so many years and my fellow kirtan wallahs: Anjula, Devadas, Nina, Sharada, and Shyama. Deep love to my family for their continuous love and support: Dad, Billinski, Mary, and my rock, Spencer.

This book was supported by so many dear friends and colleagues. Huge thanks to Joy Harris and Adam Reed for representing me,

Charlie Cox for his gorgeous mantra artwork contributions, Amishi Jha for her scientific expertise, Manorama and Kurt Lindsey for their Sanskrit expertise, and Sarah Tomlinson for her connections and inspiration. Endless gratitude to Alex Deleuse, for taking me through the writing of this book with countless hours of support, and of course, the sun and moon. Last, but not least, thank you to my editor, Kate Zimmermann, for bringing me onto this project and supporting me every step of the way.

Acknowledgments

ABOUT THE AUTHOR

Lily Cushman is a teacher, writer, and musician based in Brooklyn. Raised in Boise, Idaho with a rugged, yet sophisticated understanding of life, Lily studied music from a young age, eventually moving east to attend the Berklee College of Music as an undergraduate. There, she embarked on a lifelong journey studying yoga and meditation, seeking a more connected and holistic way of life. For the next ten years, Lily built a career as a musician, vocalist, producer, and audio engineer in Boston and New York City. However successful her work, the volatility of the music industry gradually led her to burn out and, in 2007, Lily began shifting gears to focus on teaching yoga and meditation full time.

In 2010, Lily co-founded the Brooklyn Yoga School, a donation-based yoga center voted "Best of New York" by *NY Magazine*, where she currently serves as director. For over a decade, Lily has offered yoga, meditation, and chanting events in the greater New York area, and currently serves as chief of staff to world-renowned meditation teacher, Sharon Salzberg. Lily's teachings are a synthesis of the ancient body-practices of Classical Yoga, the heart-practices of Bhakti Yoga, and the mind-practices of Insight Meditation. Expertly combined through 20 years of daily practice and study, her teachings provide an accessible pathway for awakened living in the 21st century. *A Little Bit of Mantras: An Introduction to Sacred Sounds* is her first book. For more information, music, writing, and a list of events, visit her website at www.lilycushman.com.

INDEX